FLYING YOUR BUSINESS

LEADERSHIP LESSONS FROM THE COCKPIT

FRED CALDWELL

elevate

Editorial Content: AnnaMarie McHargue
Additional Writing: Emily Sarver
Cover Designer: Arthur Cherry
Interior Layout: Leslie Hertling

Published by Elevate Publishing, Boise, ID

Printed in the United States of America

ISBN: 978-1937498597

07 08 09 10 9 8 7 6 5 4 3 2 1

Library of Congress Cataloging-in-Publication Data

DEDICATION

This book is dedicated to all leaders of organizations who desire to inspire the people they are called to guide in a positive and effective manner. The role of leader can be, as is often stated, a lonely position with the weight of many decisions placed solely on the leader's shoulders. The weight of making quality decisions that lead in the right path can be daunting. I am thankful for all the leaders I have known and the examples I have witnessed in so many settings from business to ministries of great leaders. The greatest leader I have known is Jesus Christ and His lessons of forgiveness, mercy, grace and love are the greatest example to follow.

To God be the glory!

TABLE OF CONTENTS

Ready for Takeoff

The book you are about to read is the culmination of many years thinking about the relationship between piloting and leading an organization. I have been a private pilot for over 16 years and have been the CEO and founder of a number of businesses. Over the years, the passion for leading and helping others has been at the heart of my purpose here on earth. As I have grown in leadership experiences as well as had the opportunity to work with many outstanding leaders, I have seen common themes that are somewhat easy to teach and to emulate. Likewise, as a pilot, I have learned through both expert instruction and experience how to fly an airplane and achieve intended missions. The parallels between piloting and leadership have become more clear over the years. On long flights, I would often make notes about the subject, writing notes about the application of a particular piloting strategy to our businesses. Thus began the idea for writing a book to capture what amounts to years of notes I have taken about the subject of leadership and flying—many made while flying from one place to another.

My fascination with flying began as a young boy. Planes flying overhead have always intrigued me. I often wondered where the planes were headed and what it might be like to actually be at the controls of something that could take a person to so many amazing places. At the age of seven, I began making model airplanes, which were flown on line controls. My brother and I would make planes and often crash them by poor piloting—an early lesson on the value of learning to "lead" the airplane well or pay the price of having to spend hours rebuilding the model with wood and glue. I also enjoyed making paper airplanes like the one shown on the cover of this book.

When I was a young boy, my father was a Presbyterian pastor at a church in Hamilton, Texas—a small central Texas town. The church was an older red brick building with wood pews in the sanctuary and an elevated pulpit that was three or four feet higher than the pews. As a very active young boy, it was my custom during church to busy myself by taking the church bulletin and creating some new paper airplane design. Each week, my brother and I would make a new model and then go outside after church and give them a test flight. One week, I built a model that was particularly interesting; in fact, 47 years later, I can still recall that particular paper plane. It was, in my mind, perhaps the perfect combination of wingspan, weight and length—all critical factors in building paper planes that will fly for extended periods of time. As I studied the paper plane that Sunday morning, I recall the urge to give the plane an immediate test flight rather than wait for church to end. My father was in the pulpit preaching a sermon and the plane was neatly folded to perfection—a work of art it seemed, and it so desired to fly. Burdened with the desire to allow the plane to experience the freedom of flight, I raised my arm with a well-practiced throwing motion and sent the plane on its way, aimed directly at my father in the pulpit. As expected, the plane performed amazingly well, hanging in the air long enough for my father to stop his sermon and take note of the paper airplane making lazy circles through the sanctuary.

His eye went from the plane to his family and then to his youngest son, whom he knew was the likely culprit. I gave him a look that confirmed his suspicions, and when the airplane landed he asked that I come join him in the pulpit. Never before had my father stopped in the middle of a sermon and addressed anyone, much less me. I slowly got out of the pew and went up the steps to the pulpit, where my father sat me down on a bench behind the pulpit where I could not do further harm. I actually do not recall any other ramifications from my dad—he was one of the kindest and loving men I have ever known. After the service, I did recover the airplane and, as I suspected, the plane was the best plane I had ever built—it flew great! The photo on the cover of this book is a tie to my childhood fascination with aviation coupled now with the role of leading a number of organizations.

From that early start in aviation, I always hoped that one day I would become a pilot. Thanks to my wife's support and affirmation of that dream, I was able to obtain a pilot's license in 1998 after years of working in the business world. The ability to fly and pilot a plane is a great privilege. Some people fly out of obligation to a job or to fulfill a need, but for some, flying is a calling that has been in the person's heart since their youth. For me, I always fell into the latter category.

Flying has its inherent risks and can be particularly punitive to the pilot who makes poor decisions. In many hobbies, amateurs learn to play a sport or play an instrument with little downside risk. Making a mistake may cause one to lose a game or hit the wrong note, but in flying, a significant mistake can literally cost one their life along with any passengers aboard the flight. General aviation pilots are the amateurs in flying and they have a much higher accident rate than commercial airline pilots. In fact, according to the National Transportation Safety Board, the general aviation accident rate is six times higher than for small commuter airlines and forty times higher than for transport category or commercial airlines. General aviation averages 1500 accidents a year with more than 400 pilots and passengers killed annually. The fact is, amateur flying is dangerous and not an activity to be taken lightly.

Over the years, I have been an avid reader of flying-related books and magazines. In most flying articles, the issue of accidents is a common theme. The goal in reviewing accidents is always the same— to gather what can be learned from an accident so as to prevent a future reoccurrence. The number one cause of general aviation accidents is "pilot error." From 2001 to 2011, the number one cause of fatal general aviation accidents was "loss of control," which is clearly a pilot error. The reality is that very few aircraft accidents are caused by mechanical issues. Those that do involve mechanical issues, in many cases, could have been averted with different pilot decision making.

The bottom line in flying is that the pilot, in almost all cases, makes the difference in whether a plane will accomplish the mission safely. Likewise, the CEO or top organizational leader is critical to whether or not an organization is able to accomplish the firm's mission. In his book *Good to Great*, noted author Jim Collins found that the great companies in their study had leaders at the helm with a paradoxical combination of great resolve and true humility. Collins came to call these leaders "Level 5" leaders. Great pilots are similar to the Level 5 leaders Collins describes. Such pilots are very good at managing the systems and responsibilities inherent in flying and yet also have the humility to say no to certain flights, conditions and even when they themselves are not fit to fly.

The remainder of this book is dedicated to providing you with ideas and thoughts that will help improve your leadership decision making and keep you from making decisions that might be fatal to those you are called to lead. I know that "fatal" may seem like extreme language when speaking in terms of leading a business or organization, but the reality is even if you are not a pilot, the results of poor decision making by the CEO or organizational leader (I will use the term CEO through the book to stand for the organizational leader) can be fatal to the organization. No question that the loss of a company or organization is not even close to the loss of a life but the reality is that poor decision making which leads to the loss of work by those under your leadership can have long-term, negative implications. Conversely, the way in which you lead can have long-term positive effects on those you work with and their families. The responsibility for flying the business extends well past ourselves and has with it a fiduciary for the life and welfare of our passengers (our employees) and their families. Finally, the lessons and ideas shared in this book are applicable to anyone—regardless of title—called to lead an organization or group of people. Leadership is not defined by titles but rather by the person called to lead.

In the following pages, you will read about a number of flying accidents that led to numerous fatalities. Death is a very sad thing, never part of God's plan, and therefore I do not take the accident information lightly or the impact to families that have lost loved ones. My hope is that the reader will see the issues related to each accident and be able to draw usable lessons from the accidents that may help them lead not only in business or an organization but also in the family.

So put on your seatbelt, make sure the cabin doors are locked and let's take off as we take a look at some of the lessons I have learned throughout my 30-year career in business and leading organizations.

Chapter 1

The Thanksgiving Flight

Between the busyness of leading a growing real estate company and the role of husband, parent, church and community leader, the newly-minted IFR (instrument flight rules) pilot had worked hard to earn his instrument rating. Condensing his training into a one-month period, the pilot felt a boost in his confidence as he learned the skills for flying in instrument conditions (that is, flying by reference only to the instruments in the cockpit as opposed to looking outside for reference) and, as importantly, how to operate within the FAA control system. Upon completing the rating and FAA test ride, the business owner was proud to be an instrument-rated pilot, able to operate his plane in inclement weather within the air traffic control system. He felt the instrument rating provided a great level of insurance against any major flying issue and that the rating substantiated his ability to fly the airplane in a safe manner regardless of most weather conditions. Statistics do prove that instrument-rated pilots have a much lower accident rate than non-instrument rated pilots, reflected by lower insurance rates. With more than 200 hours of flying under his belt and feeling he had just acquired the quintessential insurance policy against making a major flying error, the new pilot was extremely confident.

This confidence, however, brought with it a downside—the false sense of security found both in flying and in business. Statistics have shown that pilots are most dangerous to themselves and others when they have between 1 and 300 hours of flying time. Under 100 hours, much of the flying is typically done with an instructor, but the reality is that learning to fly is dangerous and, accordingly, a high percentage of general aviation accidents occur with pilots who have less than 100 hours of total time. Pilots who have between 100 and 300 hours oftentimes develop a false sense of confidence, believing they are truly veterans of the skies capable of handling virtually anything. That dangerous mindset has led to numerous fatal accidents. With a similar mindset, on November 21, 2001, the pilot and business owner loaded his single engine Cessna 177 with his wife, two daughters and baggage, to fly from their home in Houston to a small community outside of Tyler in East Texas for an early Thanksgiving with the pilot's parents and other family members.

The short flight from Houston to East Texas was uneventful. The pilot landed at a private airstrip located in the community where his parents lived. Surrounded by towering, majestic East Texas pine trees, the airfield was similar to many other private airstrips, with one runway and few amenities. Although he had driven to the community many times, he hadn't ever landed at that private airstrip. In command of his own plane, the pilot felt a great sense of accomplishment that day, as the wheels touched down and his mother and father arrived to meet the plane and welcome his family.

While the Thanksgiving meal was a great family experience with the pilot's family all enjoying stories and watching football on television, the pilot was distracted. Throughout the day, he contemplated the effects of a strong cold front that was to blow through on Thursday evening. The pilot also considered a second issue: the takeoff weight of his plane. He again would be flying with his two daughters, wife and baggage, but this time would be in need of more fuel, as the next leg to College Station, Texas, would take about 90 minutes of flying time, assuming no head winds. Given the amount of weight the pilot would be carrying and the fuel required to complete the fight with allowance for reserves, the plane would be at maximum weight upon takeoff. That evening, the pilot carefully filled the tanks to exactly the maximum fuel that would allow the plane to remain inside the prescribed weight and balance requirements. The diligent pilot worked to ensure the plane would not be overweight, particularly because the relatively short runway was surrounded on one end by those towering pine trees.

After a nice visit with his family, the following morning the pilot went to the airport and loaded the luggage into the plane. His wife and children would soon be arriving in another car, so he had time to consider further the flight at hand. While he was excited to get to College Station to attend the annual football matchup between the state's two biggest rivals—Texas A&M University and University of Texas—he also had some apprehension, as he noted the winds increasing substantially as the front made its way through the area. Undeterred, the pilot (also a former Texas A&M University football player) forged ahead with his flight plans. He was determined to make the game and arrive there in his own airplane—an ego-fueled decision. Once his wife and children arrived and boarded the plane, the cold front had arrived in full force and bringing with it howling winds and strong gusts. The front produced 30-knot direct crosswinds— winds running perpendicular to the runway. Such winds can create directional issues on takeoff, particularly if there are obstacles to be avoided (keep in mind the towering pine trees mentioned above) and if the airplane is heavily loaded (note the four people and baggage in a single engine, 1974 Cessna).

To that point, the pilot never had taken off in such significant crosswinds, but he somewhat disregarded them. They were coming out of the north, and the College Station airport had a north/south runway, which would eliminate the crosswinds on landing. Pilots learn early in training the difficulty of landing with a crosswind and often practice the skills required to keep the airplane centered on the runway when the winds are blowing across it. The pilot not only considered himself well accomplished at landing in crosswinds, but also, as an avid aviation reader, had never read anything that cited the dangers associated with *taking off* in significant crosswinds. He simply assumed (due to the aforementioned lack of experience) that the crosswinds would pose minimal issue on takeoff. He was ignorant of his own weaknesses, not understanding that he lacked the experience or knowledge to make a certain decision. This is opposed to stupidity, which is making the wrong decision in the face of experience or knowledge to the contrary. In this case, the pilot's ignorance, coupled with ego and a "need" to be at the game in time for kickoff, set the wheels in motion for a very bad outcome.

With the plane fully loaded with his two beautiful daughters in the backseat and lovely wife in the front seat, the pilot taxied the airplane to the end of the east/west runway. The wind blew hard out of the north, directly across the runway from the left. He chose an easterly heading for the takeoff, both to avoid power lines and also because it appeared the easterly direction had a bit of a headwind. Little did he know at the time that the easterly takeoff was a very fortunate decision for a totally different reason—God had intervened in his decision making

4

and provided an escape route for what would be a very close call. The pilot, his wife and children each wore a headset with a microphone so that they could talk to one another during the flight. After a run up (check of all the systems and engine operation), he applied full power and held the brakes for a few seconds to try to minimize the takeoff roll. Worrying about the pine trees that surrounded the runway on the east end, the pilot wanted to climb above the trees quickly. Not wanting to alarm his family or appear to lack any competency for the flight at hand (note again the emotional impact of having a new instrument rating), the pilot did not share his concerns with his wife and children. He simply acted like all was normal despite the gnawing inner voice in his head saying something was amiss.

As the plane rumbled down the runway at maximum weight and began to lift off, the pilot immediately felt the magnitude of the crosswind as the wind tried to blow the airplane to the right of the runway. Keeping the airplane centered on the runway was essential due to the pine trees that flanked the runway on both sides, starting about the midpoint of the runway and running all the way to its eastern end. To keep the airplane centered, the pilot instinctively chose the same technique used by many pilots when landing with a crosswind. He banked the airplane to the left by turning the yoke to the left and then pushed the right rudder with his right foot to keep the nose of the airplane centered on the runway. Thus the airplane was banked to the left (left wing low and right wing high) yet flying fairly straight along the runway center. The airplane was in what is known as a cross-controlled attitude, which is perfectly acceptable when landing and close to the runway when dealing with a crosswind. But during a takeoff, this is a very dangerous way to control the plane. The pilot thought little about the dangers of controlling the airplane in this manner, as he was completely focused on gaining altitude to get above the trees. It was not until much later that the pilot realized the risk he took to keep the airplane centered on the runway heading.

While the airplane managed to gain enough lift to rise slightly above the trees, it was struggling mightily to climb, as indicated by the blaring of the stall horn. A stall was imminent, as the plane had little forward speed due to the cross-controlled attitude and climb rate needed to climb above the tree level. As the plane was being buffeted by the howling wind coming from the left, the plane seemed to be hovering above the towering trees with almost no forward speed for what seemed minutes. With the plane suspended in the narrow gap between flying and losing all lift by falling into a stall, the pilot searched for options that might enable the airplane to gain speed. The balance of the pilot and his family's lives hung on every blaring sound made by the stall horn. All the pilot could hear through his headset was the labored breathing of his wife and children as the plane struggled to climb.

After the flight, the pilot would come to understand and fully believe that God stepped in that fateful day and held the plane above the trees for the seconds necessary for him to see His escape route. At the eastern end of the runway, obscured behind all the pine trees, was a lake set in a valley well below the airport elevation. The lake was probably a mile long and the valley perhaps several miles long. Once clear of the trees and upon seeing the drop in terrain and the familiar lake, the pilot immediately pushed the airplane nose down and dove toward the lake. The result was increasing airspeed, which silenced the stall horn and allowed the plane to gain the flow of air over the wings to fly as designed. The valley was truly God-given.

Had the pilot departed to the west where the terrain was flat to rising, the outcome would have likely been the death of the entire family.

The takeoff was a terrifying event, with all passengers that day knowing that something had been terribly wrong as the plane hovered over the trees. Although the pilot was horrified by the decisions he had made, he did not fully comprehend the gravity of what had happened. His mind and ego required that he minimize the risk to his family and to act as though he had the situation in perfect control—which could not have been further from the truth. As often happens in flying and in life, one problem leads to another, particularly when the problem is not acknowledged.

As the plane gained altitude and headed toward College Station, a new issue appeared—turbulence. The turbulence left behind from the strong front passing through the region was jarring and very uncomfortable for all aboard. After the takeoff and departure experience, the discomfort from the turbulence was highly amplified as emotions were at a high pitch for everyone in the plane. The pilot could feel his wife's fear and resentment growing as they traveled toward College Station. The pilot's wife did not like flying in general, yet like many women, she trusted her husband to make quality, safe flying decisions. She had agreed to fly to east Texas that weekend with trust and confidence in her husband as a pilot, a trust that shrunk with each turbulent mile as the plane bounced along toward their destination.

A third and very serious issue now became apparent: the wind that was expected to be a slight tailwind for the trip turned into a headwind. *Strike three!* Shortly into the flight it became apparent that the winds were not as forecast and the ample fuel reserve would now be down to minimums. Given that the skies were clear and there were a number of alternate airports along the route, the pilot chose to defer a decision on the fuel issue and proceed as filed. However, the fuel situation was about to move from minimums to critical.

The two largest universities in Texas were playing the most watched and attended game in the state, a game where alumni and public officials from all over the state fly private planes into Easterwood Airport (located adjacent to the Texas A&M Campus)—a fact the pilot had not considered in his planning. As the pilot approached College Station, the air traffic controller directed the pilot to turn to the west away from College Station so he could work the flight into the stream of landing airplanes. While the plane headed west away from the destination, the pilot watched the fuel indicators continue to decline. Monitoring his watch, the pilot had a designated landing time, which would allow the plane to land with the minimum fuel reserves. However, now as the flight moved away from the airport and the designated landing time was only minutes away, the pilot began to sweat once again. He had put his family in yet another major predicament: fuel exhaustion. His mind raced with thoughts about how to best remedy the problem—including eyeing potential landing spots in the Texas fields should the engine quit due to fuel exhaustion. Even though his fuel calculations showed that he had time remaining, it is never comforting to be in a plane when the fuel gauges are nearing the low fuel warnings.

Private airplane fuel gauges are reference gauges only, as the pilot must determine fuel quantities and fuel burn based on time. However, when the fuel indicators start nearing the low fuel point, it is very unsettling regardless of calculations. The mind begins to ponder whether the engine is burning the calculated gallons per hour or not. In the plane the pilot was flying at the time, there was no effective way to know exactly how much fuel truly remained. Even with today's new electronic fuel systems, the pilot must still program the amount of fuel upon takeoff and the system must accurately measure the fuel burn— both of which can be inaccurate.

As the controller continued to direct the flight westward, the pilot asked the controller for a turn back to Easterwood, hoping the controller would sense in his voice a need to land. Not only did the controller not grant the request but instead gave the pilot holding instructions for a point much farther west. Controllers give holding instructions to pilots that may require the pilot to fly to a specific area and then fly an oval pattern around that point in space, known as a "fix." In a sense, the holding pattern acts as an aerial parking lot, giving the controllers time to direct planes into an airport or perform some other function while a plane or planes are held circling points in the sky. In this case, the hold was the final straw in a very tense morning of flying. The pilot could not believe his ears when the controller issued the hold command. He was getting low on fuel, he had already put his family at significant risk once that day due to his poor decision making, and now he was about to put his family at risk again.

The pilot repeated the controller's hold command (standard pilot communication is to repeat a controller's command exactly) and then pondered options. Should he request another airport? Should he cancel the IFR (instrument flight rules) flight plan and go by visual flight rules (VFR) into Easterwood? Should he declare an emergency with the controller and confess his concerns over low fuel? Should he say nothing and pray that God would again rescue him and, more importantly, his loved ones from another predicament? After considering the options, the pilot took a hybrid approach and called the controller and told him he was low on fuel and needed to land as soon as possible. One of the things the pilot had learned over life is the value of confession—coming into agreement with God over the errors of his way. Confessing brings healing to the soul and seems to yield good fruit no matter how painful the moment of confession may be. In this case, the very busy controller chose to somewhat ignore the situation and asked the pilot to continue flight to the hold. Now the pilot was even more perplexed on how to proceed, with the fuel gauges continuing their decline and the 45-minute reserve landing time rapidly approaching.

As the plane arrived at the waypoint to begin the hold, the controller issued the command to turn back toward the airport and begin the approach. Instead of making the plane park in the sky, the controller, perhaps in light of the low-fuel confession, gave the very positive news that the plane could now fly to the destination! As the pilot flew toward College Station and prepared to land, the pilot pondered exactly how much fuel really did remain in the tanks. He knew that he was likely inside the 45-minute reserve but was not sure that the actual fuel would match his calculations.

The descent into College Station at lower altitudes was again very turbulent, and as the plane bounced and rocked its way into the final landing sequence, he could feel his wife's fear and anxiety with each bump. She had said little during the trip, but he knew she was very unhappy with her husband for putting their children in grave danger multiple times that day. Once on the ground and parked, the pilot's wife literally jumped out of the plane and expressed her built-up fear and disappointment in her husband for endangering the lives of their family. And she was right. He had made poor decisions more than once that day, and they nearly cost him his family.

I was the pilot of that flight. In hindsight, it is almost inconceivable that I would have made the decisions I did on that fateful day. Years of perspective have allowed me to assess more accurately my mental condition and arrogance in deciding to make the flight. With 500 additional hours and hundreds of subsequent flights, my pilot decision making has improved substantially and experience now affords me improved understanding of the risks I took that Thanksgiving flight. To lose my family over my error in decision making is almost more than I can think about still today—14 years later. To ensure that I never repeat the same sequence of decisions, I, over the years, have replayed that day and the events leading up to my decision to take off. Ultimately, I was responsible for my family and their safety—there was only one pilot that day. There was only one person responsible for setting the vision and plan for getting our family from east Texas to College Station. There was only one person who could have made the decision to cancel the plan—me. My passengers put their trust in me. They believed in me and my decision making. Yet I failed the ones I love most on this earth.

In effect, I was the CEO of that flight, and I failed miserably. Truly, by the grace of God, our family is alive today. When that plane was hovering over the pine trees with the stall horn blaring, the results could have been fatal. Stalls are generally not a major issue for a pilot when given enough altitude to recover, but the danger of a stall increases greatly when near the ground where recovery time is very limited. When an airplane stalls it loses some amount of altitude as the pilot, in general, must level the wings, lower the nose and add power to increase airflow over the wings to restore the lost lift. In my fateful takeoff, I had the plane in a cross-controlled attitude, which further adds to the recovery process. Had the plane actually stalled, with

11

the manner in which I was controlling the airplane, it immediately would have dropped a wing, rolled over on its back and spiraled to the ground. There would have been no possible recovery given our low altitude and lack of forward speed. Only a few knots of air speed separated the plane from a full, cross-controlled stall—I was only a few knots away from killing my beautiful wife and daughters. I still shudder at the thought of that day. (It is important to note that no time in any previous training had any instructor discussed this particular situation or the negative impact of cross-controlling the plane on takeoff. In fact, to this day, I still have never seen an aviation article written on the subject.)

After the football game, my wife was so rattled that she, understandably, refused to fly back to Houston with me. She and the girls drove home with friends, while I walked several miles from the stadium to the airport (a time to think as I walked), eventually flying back to Houston on my own. That time alone allowed me to thank God for keeping us all alive, to reflect upon the numerous mistakes of the day and to contemplate how to avoid ever ending up in any similar situation, whether in flying or in other aspects of life.

Chapter 2

The CEO Factor

If I had crashed the plane on that Friday in 2001, the results obviously would have been my fault. While the FAA and others might have cited the weather or other contributing factors for the flight's failure, ultimately I was responsible for making the decision to take off that fateful morning. Likewise, as CEO, I am ultimately responsible for whether our organization moves ahead to achieve our stated vision and mission or whether the firm struggles to gain altitude and risks crashing into the ground. Typically there are several factors involved in the failure of a company, with the CEO or organization head being only one of them. Managers can make costly mistakes; team members can fail to follow through on assignments; external economic factors can affect sales; and hundreds of other scenarios can cause good companies to go under. But the CEO takes responsibility for the key issues that determine whether an organization succeeds or fails. Critical leadership items such as setting vision, determining corporate strategies, hiring key people and sourcing the capital necessary to complete the mission (part of the "fuel") while "piloting" the organization are much like the issues faced by the pilot of a plane. The roles are very similar, and much can be learned from piloting strategies and from piloting errors that can help improve our decision making when called to lead others.

In his 2001 book *Good to Great*, author Jim Collins and his 21-person research team spent five years sorting through a list of 1,435 companies, looking for those that, over time, made substantial improvements in their performance. In the quest to find good companies that managed to move into the "great" category, Collins and his researchers read and coded 6,000 articles, generated more than 2,000 pages of interview transcripts and created 384 megabytes of computer data. Among other things, one discovery found in the heart of those rare and truly great companies was a corporate culture that rigorously sought and promoted those people who thought and acted in a disciplined manner. And in the study of great companies, mediocre organizations and poor performing companies, Collins concluded—despite attempts to find examples where this was not the case—the CEO of the organization ultimately set the tone of the corporate culture and was the most important individual in determining whether a company would become a great company. The CEO truly acts as the pilot of the organization and must make daily decisions that will either move an organization to greatness or toward mediocrity or even failure.

In a 2003 article in *Fortune* magazine, Collins identified people like Sam Walton (Walmart during the 1970s and '80s), David Packard (Hewlett-Packard in the 1940s and '50s), Katherine Graham (*The Washington Post* during Watergate in the 1970s), James Burke (Johnson & Johnson in the 1970s and '80s), Darwin Smith (Kimberly-Clark in the 1970s) and Bill Allen (Boeing in the 1940s and '50s) as some of the greatest CEOs in the history of American business. They were courageous, visionary, tone-setting men and women whose decisions—

often under duress—positively shaped the future direction of their companies.

Burke's decision to pull Tylenol capsules off the shelves in response to the cyanide-poisoning crisis of 1982 resulted in Johnson & Johnson taking a $100-million hit to earnings. But it also earned national respect, praise and adulation for the company and for Burke as he led the J&J response to the act of terrorism. Pulling Tylenol clearly showed that at J&J, customer safety outweighed short-term financial concerns. But Collins points out that Burke's defining moment actually occurred three years earlier when he pulled 20 key executives into a room and thumped his finger on a copy of the J&J credo. Penned 36 years earlier by R.W. Johnson, Jr., it stated that J&J held itself to a higher duty and responsibility than other brands, because it owed that sense of purpose to "mothers and all others who use our products." Burke worried that by the 1970s, executives had come to view the credo as an interesting artifact but hardly relevant to the day-to-day challenges of American capitalism.

"I said, 'Here's the credo. If we're not going to live by it, let's tear it off the wall,'" Burke later told Joseph Badaracco and Richard Ellsworth for their book *Leadership and the Quest for Integrity*. "We either ought to commit to it or get rid of it." The team sat there a bit stunned, wondering if Burke was serious. He was, and the room erupted into a debate that ended with a recommitment. Burke and his colleagues would conduct similar meetings around the world, restoring the credo as a living document, which prepared the company to handle the crisis of 1982.

Perhaps Bill Allen's story is most fitting for a book on aviation. Boeing's planes helped win World War II. But the Allied Forces' victory in 1945 could have doomed Boeing. Revenues plummeted more than

90 percent as orders for bombers vanished overnight. Bombers were the essence of business at Boeing—at least until Allen assumed control of the company on September 1, 1945, following the death of former president Philip Johnson. Allen never viewed Boeing as only a bomber company. In 1952 he bet heavily on a new commercial jet, the 707, even though potential customers scoffed at the notion that Boeing would ever enter the commercial aviation industry. Under Allen's leadership, however, Boeing built the 707, 727, 737, and 747—four of the most successful commercial airliners in history. At a board meeting described by Robert Serling in his *Legend and Legacy: The Story of Boeing and Its People,* a director said that if the 747 was too big for the market to swallow, Boeing could back out. "Back out?" stiffened Allen. "If the Boeing Aircraft Company says we will build this airplane, we will build it even if it takes the resources of the entire company."

"Like today's CEOs, [he] endured the swarming gnats who think small: short time frames, pennies per share, a narrow purpose," Collins wrote of Allen. "Allen thought bigger...and left a legacy to match."

Of course, there is also the other end of the CEO spectrum. Each year, the business world is filled with examples of companies of all sizes that crashed because their pilot/CEO failed to recognize warning signs, failed to exhibit common sense or failed his employees, investors or customers in some other way. Sydney Finkelstein, a professor at Dartmouth College's Tuck School of Business and author of *Why Smart Executives Fail,* annually compiles an interesting list of the worst CEOs from the previous year. "If failure really is a better teacher than success, then we're wasting a chance to learn from the corporate world's many management mistakes if we don't study glaring examples of business leadership gone wrong," Finkelstein wrote in December 2012.

The point is that even very sharp people who have risen to the top of their profession after years of hard work are susceptible to making decisions that ultimately crash an organization. Sometimes those decisions are based on ignorance. As in my case of taking off with a significant crosswind and not giving proper thought to the external factors, so many CEOs are forced into similar unknown situations and must take decisive actions to prevent their organizations from crashing. One of the keys to avoiding a crash, I believe, is the mindset of the leader. As in piloting, the arrogant and prideful leader that has things "figured out" (particularly when they are low in actual experience) is at the most risk. Like me feeling a bit bulletproof because of my new instrument rating in 2000, so is the young, inexperienced leader who has had some years of success running a business unit and is handed the keys to the entire company as its CEO. Organizational leaders with both limited experience *and* type A personalities can be a recipe for failure. In contrast, wise leaders are able to evaluate their own weaknesses and see clearly their need for good judgment while still moving the organization forward. Such wisdom is often the result of many years of experience. Thus the smart leader is wise to seek out the counsel of those with much more experience.

As leaders, to avoid taking off into conditions that will put an organization at risk, we must not become so enamored or obsessed with reaching a destination that we allow ourselves and those around us to face the possibility of total loss. Make no mistake: great leaders indeed take smart, calculated risks that often may be seen by others as highly risky, but the wise leader has evaluated those risks and has a plan for addressing them. Unlike my flight into life-threatening conditions, the wise leader evaluates the environment and has contingency plans in place to maneuver the organization in a manner designed to reduce risk while still achieving the objective. As leaders, we are the pilots of our organizations, responsible for providing vision and direction. We cannot always avoid turbulent conditions, but we can steer clear of many storms by learning from our own experiences and the experiences of others. The Bible states in Proverbs 15:22 that "plans fail for lack of counsel but with many advisors they succeed." Great leaders seek out the counsel of others.

I believe there are proven, time-tested flying principles that have evolved over the history of flight—many driven from historic accidents—that can be applied to success in leadership. Most flying accidents become the catalysts for improving flying safety. The FAA, commercial airlines and general aviation organizations like AOPA are leading the way in developing training, procedures and strategies to prevent similar accidents. Stated differently, these training exercises, procedures and strategies are developed to help ensure flight missions are completed and not interrupted by a similar accident. The goal of any organization should include completing stated missions. Thus, like flying, intentional approaches should be developed to ensure mission completion, both in the air and in your organization. As mentioned previously, the primary key to successfully completing a flight mission or leading an organization is the pilot/leader. In this regard, the following chapters detail key principles relating directly to the role of pilot/CEO/leader.

Chapter 3

CEO Temperament

Great leaders are well aware of their limitations and especially the limitations of their own temperament. Consider temperament and its possible role in decision making for the pilot of the following two crashes:

The pilot crashed his plane the first time after obtaining only 34 total flying hours. The aircraft he was flying at the time was a Beech A36, which is not typically flown by a beginning pilot, as the plane is a high speed, retractable gear model generally used by experienced pilots.

The pilot's first accident occurred while flying from Stockton to Torrance (a 300-nautical-mile route he had repeatedly flown previously, despite lacking instructor approval). There was a low cloud ceiling over Torrance that forced the pilot to backtrack 10 minutes to Van Nuys, which was long enough to deplete the aircraft's available fuel. The pilot then crash-landed his airplane in a backyard—in the dark. By great fate the pilot was not killed and he walked away from a night landing with the engine out. He was very fortunate.

Despite such a brush with fate, this particular pilot proceeded without seemingly any real education as to the dangers in not planning appropriately when flying. Just three months later, the pilot had obtained another Beechcraft and then finished his private pilot license. He went on to log almost 300 hours in the new plane during that year.

Fifteen months after the first crash, the pilot and his wife departed Torrance, this time headed for Palm Springs. Despite the short flight distance (92 nautical miles), the route was complicated by the need to navigate through the Banning Pass. This pass spans 19 miles and sits at an elevation of 2,000 feet between two mountain peaks on either side that reach elevations of 11,500 feet and 10,800 feet respectively.

Twenty-seven minutes into the flight, the pilot asked the TRACON controller if he was on course through the pass, indicating he could not see the mountain peaks. At the point of his communication with the controller, the pilot was only eight miles away from the pass and his cruising altitude was 7,500 feet, which put him a good distance below the peaks. These same peaks are visible from Los Angeles, over 100 miles from where they stand, unless they are hidden by cloud cover. Such was the case on this fateful day for the non-instrument rated pilot—he was evidently flying in the clouds with no clarity on where his plane was relative to the mountain pass or the adjacent peaks—not a good place to be.

The pilot's brief communication with the TRACON controller would be his last. His plane impacted Mt. San Jacinto at 7,600 feet and was completely destroyed. The first accident was not enough to diminish his overconfidence, and obstructed his good judgment, making him believe he could navigate blindly through the cloud-obstructed pass.

The pilot in the above accident clearly did not appreciate the risks he was taking even after surviving, only months before, a crash landing at night into a wooded area. He seemingly failed to learn from his own poor planning and pressed ahead into other dangerous situations, the last of which claimed not only his own life but also that of his wife.

Why do individuals take such risks and allow themselves to make amazingly poor decisions? Many times (perhaps most), the temperament of the pilot/leader is at the root of the issue.

Temperament is an interesting topic to consider during a discussion on CEO leadership. Flying history, as noted in the article above, has long shown that poor flying decisions are often actually related to the pilot's temperament. So what do I mean when using the word "temperament"? When I use "temperament," I am using the word to describe the God-given wiring that a person has had since birth. Unlike some, I believe and have witnessed through my life that we are all uniquely wired for a purpose, and that such purpose has to do with the roles we will play in life. Our God-given wiring can and does significantly impact our approach to leadership in an organization and certainly when acting as the pilot of an airplane.

For many years, our company has used the DISC assessment, both as part of the interview process and with our team members, as a means to improve teamwork and communication. The DISC assessment, which is based upon theories developed by noted psychologist William Moulton Marston, is a simple, 24-question test that is taken in less than 15 minutes. The questionnaire appears very benign to the person taking it and therefore one would expect the results to be rather simplistic. The assessment results, however, are provided in highly detailed and comprehensive reports that accurately describe the person's decision-making style, ideal environment, areas of weakness, strengths and other key details all tied to what some psychologists refer to as predictable personality traits and outward behaviors. I believe these predictable personality traits and outward

21

behaviors are closely aligned with a person's temperament. Therefore, for the rest of the book, I will use the term "temperament" to describe the predictable personality traits and outward behaviors.

The DISC acronym represents "D" for dominance, "I" for influencing, "S" for steadiness and "C" for conscientiousness. All four characteristics are set against an average or mean for the population of thousands who have previously taken the assessment, and the results are presented in both graphical and narrative forms. The graphical form uses a mean line that splits each of the four characteristics in half (see Figure A below) so that the person's results can be compared on a relative basis. The following graph shows my personal results so you can understand one way the results are depicted:

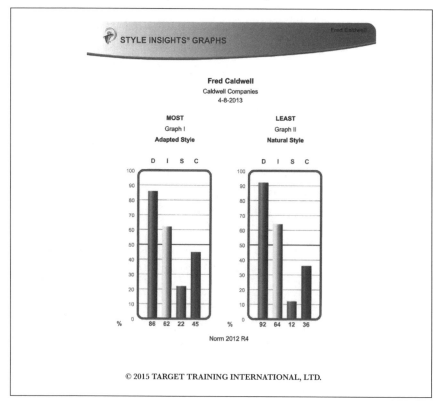

Thus, my graph depicts a high-D temperament which means my results are well "above the line" in dominance. Therefore, simply by looking at the graph, one can see that I can be a fairly dominating personality, which has both good and bad implications in leadership. I am comfortable with higher levels of risk than someone with a lower D result, perhaps below the median line. A key principle to understand is that neither the high-D nor the low-D temperament is more or less important, but such persons should likely play different roles on the team. I am always amazed when I see people with the wrong temperaments for a given role spend a career or lifetime in the "wrong seat on the bus," to quote Jim Collins. Finding the right seat on the bus means understanding our wiring and how our personal wiring can apply to different positions. Some leadership roles would best be suited to lower D personalities. Such lower-D

A key principle to understand is that neither the high-D nor the low-D temperament is more or less important, but such persons should likely play different roles on the team.

personalities may make more deliberate decisions and be more team oriented, while a high-D personality will likely make faster decisions and may act more independently. Both leadership styles can be successful; it is a matter of difference in behaviors. Again, the key is not viewing a person's temperament as wrong or right but as a means to evaluate the person's wiring for a particular role and understanding how the person may make decisions.

The next characteristic is the interpersonal area. I am what is considered a high I since my results are above the line in this section.

An above-the-line I indicates someone who is comfortable with people and likely draws their energy from people. The higher the I, the more the need for interpersonal interaction to increase sense of worth. The high-I person will work the room at a party, meeting many people, and will more easily mingle within a crowd. Some would say this describes an extroverted person, but I tend to find that the high-I person is simply comfortable around people and may or may not be significantly extroverted. The low-I person, on the other hand, will tend to be less comfortable with people, will have fewer relationships, will tend to visit with only a few people at the party but will tend to have deep, long-lasting relationships. In comparison, the high-D person may have many relationships but few that are deep. You are probably evaluating your own temperament as you read these descriptions, but I would again say that the results do not indicate a wrong or right but an idea of "fit." The fit for a high-I person is obviously to work with people while the lower I person can perform well in an environment with fewer people and, for example, may fit a more technical role than a high I person. Many engineers and accountants will tend to have below-the-line I temperaments, particularly if they prefer the technical side of the business as opposed to the client relations and business development roles. The high-I leader has less difficulty communicating with people, while the low-I leader may not enjoy large crowds but can do an outstanding job leading a small group, which requires more intimate communication and close working relationships.

The high-S person is steadier than a low-S person. The high-S person would generally prefer to finish one task before moving on to the next. The low-S person may prefer to have many projects in process at one time. The higher the S scoring, the more the person would prefer to perform a single task, while the lower the S result, the more the person will need to multi-task. I use the word "need" specifically to make a point—the less a role fits one's temperament, the more stress that person will have in their life. Thus a high-S person who is charged with a role that requires significant multi-tasking will likely find the role stressful, while a low-S person might find the role very fulfilling. However, the low-S person tends to be less detail-oriented than the high-S person and may miss critical details if such details are not perceived as being essential to the mission. My wife, Susan, is a high-S person. She is very detail-oriented and needs order in her life. She always will gravitate to a detailed plan with clear steps. Likewise, the high S will prefer a calm environment that is free of distractions. Conversely, Susan's husband, your author, is a low-S, meaning I enjoy multi-tasking. And, if there are not enough balls in the air in a given day, I will likely go kick some up just to make the juggling more interesting. I enjoy an environment with high energy and potential distractions where as my wife would much prefer calmer surroundings and less variety. Such is the natural wiring differences between Susan and me. The same is true of your team members; some are low-S and some are high-S. Both are important to the organization and should play complementing roles. Fitted to the right roles, the two together can make a great team—one more focused on detail and process while the other focuses on managing a variety of tasks.

As a footnote, the high- and low-S temperaments also relate to children as they do to adults. In my opinion, too many children are labeled as ADD and ADHD, thus implying in our society that the child's mind is incorrectly wired. I suspect, however, that many entrepreneurs, high-performing artists and other very successful people would have been labeled as ADD and ADHD if diagnosed as children. I believe it is critical as parents to affirm our children and rejoice in the fact that some of us have children that are uniquely gifted at multi-tasking (low-S) due to their God-given wiring versus labeling them as ADD or ADHD in need of medicine.

I remember as a child in second grade, the teachers put me in a "special" class by myself so I could walk a balance beam and do other focus exercises while the other students did the normal schoolwork. You see, I had a very active mind, and sitting in a classroom with straight chairs and lineal teaching styles was very challenging for me. The issue was not that my mind was incorrectly wired and needed to be changed, but rather I needed to learn in a different environment with a different style of teaching. I did not need medicine (as is commonly prescribed today) but rather had to train my mind to focus on key issues. Athletics and other endeavors in my life provided the framework of discipline needed to shape my ability to focus. The very nature of having a low-S temperament can lead to success in many endeavors—end of soapbox and back to the book (from your very low-S author).

The high-C (conscientious) person likely will be very compliant with an organization's rules and system/process oriented, while the low-C person will be much more committed to personal values and may have less regard for the organization's process. The low C more likely will be focused simply on results while the high C will desire to follow process and steps if possible. Again, the degree any one characteristic is above or below the median varies greatly from person to person, so a person may be only a bit high or low in any characteristic. In my case, my C measure is only slightly below the line, meaning I am fairly compliant with rules and procedures. I suspect my years of playing team sports had some influence on my "C" results. In football and other team sports, you learn quickly that complying with your coaches is more desirable than the pain incurred for violating their policies.

You also will note that the two bar charts are labeled "Adapted Style" and "Natural Style." The difference between the two is simply a measure of how much a person must adapt their God-given temperament to meet the requirements of their current situation. In my case, the adapted and natural charts are almost the same—reflective that the role I have in our business and other organizations is a good fit with my natural temperament. Conversely, I have interviewed many whose adapted behavior is significantly different than their natural temperament. These people usually are under much stress as they must work hard to be different than they are made to be. As a leader, it is always best to look at each team member's temperament and work to find the best fit for the person to minimize adapted behavior.

I have taken the DISC assessment several times over a 15-plus year period and have found that my test results have changed only minimally over time. The results today for my "D" are very much the same as 15 years ago. My "I" has declined some over the years, which I believe ties directly to my move out of working directly in our brokerage company many years ago and focusing my efforts fully on investment and development work. The investment and development business requires much less people interaction, which I suspect has lowered my "I" assessment results. My "S" is about the same— relatively low, indicating a mind that can move from project to project in rapid succession—and the "C" is a bit higher, meaning I am more focused on systems and process than in the past.

So how does our temperament apply to piloting and leadership? It can be said that temperament applies to all areas of our life but this is especially true in the specific area of risk taking.

Chapter 4

Risk Taking

As demonstrated by last chapter's story, risk taking can be deadly. Without proper planning and understanding of the risk, a mission can result in loss of life in piloting and loss of an organization in the case of a leader.

Risk, however, is always present and never can be fully eliminated. To accomplish anything of significance requires risk or, as I believe, faith. Faith is acting in the absence of all information. Too many times, people and organizations miss opportunities for lack of faith. Faith means that a leader will proceed with a good, objective plan even though not every outcome can be evaluated or fully known. However, the more critical the mission and the greater the downside risk, the more the leader should evaluate risk. I often have noted to my colleagues that, while important, the execution of various strategies is not "NASA critical." What I mean by the comment is that the downside risk of sending a person into space requires incredible attention to detail that is not required for most business strategies. Thus, in many cases, the risk of not acting outweighs the need for further analysis. To not act in so many cases is simply to not have faith.

In flying, each mission can be fatal to the pilot and his passengers. Thus the level of risk must be carefully addressed and the pilot must determine if he is capable of making the flight with an acceptable level of risk. Each flight clearly involves risk, as the mere act of flying an airplane involves a certain amount of risk. Once the airplane is moving forward at takeoff speed, risks of severe injury and even death are assumed. Add just a bit of altitude to the forward speed, and the pilot and occupants are now subject to the risks involved in flight. The pilot is responsible both for evaluating such risk prior to ever moving the airplane to the runway and also for ensuring that the mission can be achieved with the lowest acceptable risk.

Some leaders and pilots are addicted to the adrenaline caused by taking risk. The same personalities that jump off rocks with a parachute strapped to their backs are similar high-D personalities that will lead an organization off the cliff just for the thrill of the wind screaming by their faces. A recent accident involved a thrill-seeking executive who also happened to be a pilot. The business executive was well known for his flying exploits and had numerous type ratings in various complex airplanes. The pilot was also a successful entrepreneur who had done well in business, affording him the time and resources to pursue aviation records. His demise came while flying a rather simple plane on what amounts to a Sunday drive.

The accident occurred in a mountainous area on a clear day with no real weather issues. The entrepreneur/pilot was flying a simple to fly, single engine airplane and was likely sightseeing as he flew near the mountains. There were no witnesses to the crash, but the wreckage location would indicate the pilot, who had logged over 6,000 hours, was likely flying close to rock formations and perhaps caught a downdraft or other wind current for which the plane he was flying was not able to overcome.

The pilot had many noteworthy flying achievements that included setting a number of aviation records. With all his flying feats, he might have felt his final flight was a minor excursion, but the low-level flight in mountainous terrain had risk of its own. It is not the perceived risk or lack thereof that can bite us but the actual risk incurred in each day. Some of us have a propensity to simply accept higher levels of risk.

I never met the pilot, but I suspect that he had a very high-D temperament given his propensity for risk. We also can surmise that he had a need for excitement in his life that, like a drug, required greater and greater levels of risk to quench. The pilot had described himself as "very aggressive." The traits that had helped him build a successful business in a very competitive market segment are likely the same traits that perhaps led him to evaluate improperly the risk on the day he died flying in the mountains. Such is the case for many organizational leaders. The mundane task of running the business can, at times, be too ordinary and boring for the high-D, low-S leader (I can so relate to this issue) that such a leader may plunge

To not act in so many cases is simply to not have faith.

the organization into high-stress, challenging transactions to fulfill the leader's own need for risk. The effective high-D, low-S leader who understands their wiring needs to be aware of their built-in penchant for risk and confesses such to those around him. Such a leader needs wise counsel in close proximity to ensure that they do not lead the team into potentially lethal conditions, such as flying an airplane low over mountainous terrain.

The following four key steps can be used to reduce risk to an acceptable level and to manage our personal temperaments in a way that gives us the best opportunity to lead our organizations to success. The four key steps—planning, counsel, physical/spiritual health and speed—will be discussed in the next several chapters.

Chapter 5

Planning and the *High-D* Leader

How does a good pilot—or good leader—avoid flying into the walls of a canyon? I believe the answer lies in good planning and the consideration of one's temperament. Absent these considerations, the life of the pilot, or the success of the company, will be put in jeopardy. The following accident details a lack of planning that resulted in a tragic outcome.

It was a clear morning in late November 2004, and a CASA 212-200 (a Spanish-built utility plane) departed from Bagram Air Base in Kabul, Afghanistan, to deliver cargo to Farah, another air base about 400 miles from Kabul. Though the airplane sat nine, six were aboard, including two pilots, a mechanic, and three U.S. Army soldiers.

After takeoff, there was no radio communication, only radar detection that traced the airplane traveling on a non-standard flight path for Farah. The typical flight path avoided the highest parts of the mountain range by flying to the south and then to the west. The flight, however, headed to the north into the Bamiyan Valley region and ultimately turned south into a canyon. Upon entering the valley, the CASA faded from radar contact, but the cockpit recorder makes it clear the decision to take a non-standard route into a canyon was the captain's decision. Based on the dialogue, the captain wanted to see where the canyon led.

The recording starts as the mechanic notices that the captain is taking an unusual route to Farah. The captain remarks on the exceptional weather and visibility conditions and expresses confidence in his ability to navigate through the mountains. Though the passengers continue to question the route including the suggestion that it might be best to start a climb, the captain makes light of the comments and continues farther into the canyon with the adjacent ridges rising steadily above the airplane.

But as the canyon walls around them start to tighten, the passengers become increasingly concerned. Finally, the captain puts the aircraft into a climb but late into the game. With the surrounding ridges well above the plane, the captain puts the plane into a maximum climb attitude causing the stall horn to sound briefly. Rather than turn around (which still was possible at this point), the captain instructs his first officer to drop a quarter flaps, and the first officer indicates that their current airspeed is 95 knots. The optimal angle and climb speed for this aircraft would be 83 knots with full flaps.

The recording suddenly ends seconds later, the stall warning still persisting.

Three days later, a recovery team trudged through 20 inches of snow to follow a 450-foot debris path that would lead them to the wreckage. It rested at an altitude of 14,650 feet in a box canyon whose ridges were at 15,000 feet—the plane was only 350 feet short of clearing the canyon walls. While the team recovered the bodies of the victims and the cockpit voice recorder, they left the rest of the wreckage behind.

This kind of accident happens periodically and is unfortunately not unique. A pilot may choose to fly into a canyon to purvey the landscape more closely or to relish the excitement of flying close to the ground and adjacent mountains. Lack of planning by the unprepared pilot can lead to the demise of all onboard should there not be an effective escape route.

There are two primary reasons these pilots, and others, have lost their lives flying into box canyons: thrill and lack of planning. The need for risk coupled with a temperament that thirsts for adventure can create an opportunity for failure simply because of very poor pre-flight preparation. A critical way to help reduce risk associated with higher risk ventures—such as exploring a canyon by airplane—is to have a plan. Before flying into a canyon, the pilot should have a pre-determined, clear exit plan before a plane is ever flown into any canyon environment.

With proper planning, risk can be reduced and the mission achieved. A critical element in planning is determining non-negotiable items prior to the mission, in other words, determining what boundaries will not be crossed in achieving a particular mission. In the accident above, a simple agreement by the crew that they would not descend below 500 feet would have kept the crew out of the canyon.

Another key issue for most businesses and organizations is speed. I believe that speed can kill, but speed is a repeated theme in winning and achieving high priority objectives in competitive marketplaces. Properly planned, speed does in fact win, time and time again in business. But unplanned speed also has killed many an organization. Oftentimes, a leader foolishly forges ahead without capital, with the wrong people and without an exit strategy should the deal go south. These, along with a host of other examples, demonstrate situations in which leaders and their teams (many times comprised of other like-minded leaders) have moved ahead unprepared, in many cases, due to their high-D temperament. Even without proper preparation, the leader may be able to negotiate certain situations; however, if the environment takes an unexpected turn, then the leaders, without appropriate alternative options, may find themselves like a pilot in a box canyon with no way to climb over the surrounding mountains and not enough space to turn around.

For long-term success, urgency must be balanced with planning. The high-D personality found in many business leaders has to be offset with a commitment to quality planning if the leader is to serve the long-term interests of investors, partners and stockholders. The high-D leader may take off from a small airstrip in east Texas and risk the lives of his family, all in order to get to a football game that he cannot even recall the final score of 14 years later. Without planning controls in place, the high-D leader can put themselves and those they lead in precarious positions. One of the great benefits of understanding the DISC model is learning to understand how we are wired so that we can be more effective leaders. In my case, as a high-D individual, I have learned the value of forcing myself to slow down and evaluate the environment when the situation becomes tense.

In flying, it is the pilot's responsibility to plan the flight. Even in the beginning stages of pilot training, the pilot learns how to chart a course on paper charts that are now easily developed on GPS systems. However, it is the pilot's responsibility to determine not only the direction of flight, but also the resources that must be carried to accomplish the flight. The pilot must calculate how much fuel to carry, including required reserve fuel that must be on board should the weather or other issues delay landing at the destination airport. Too much fuel and the plane may be overweight for the required payload. Too little fuel and the pilot will be required to land short of the desired destination airport or worse, run out of fuel before reaching the intended landing point. It is the pilot's responsibility to implement the strategies that will result in a successful flight. The leader of an organization is also ultimately responsible for determining the course for their organization and the resources necessary to achieve the organizational objectives. As in a multi-crew cockpit situation, most leaders have additional and valuable leadership resources on their team, but ultimately the success or failure of the organization to achieve the desired results falls to the leader.

Therefore, planning the mission is a critical step and requires the leader to evaluate the internal capabilities of the organization and then compare those capabilities to the external environment in which the desired mission must occur. Inevitably, the final analysis of both internal and external factors for any organization falls to the CEO or top leadership. High-D leaders who neglect planning due to their natural tendency to "wing it" will put any organization in peril given unpredicted changes in internal resources or external conditions. So how should the high-D leader ensure against the natural tendency for bravado and confidence that can lead the organization into dangerous flight situations? Do what top pilots do: develop a process for the organization and stick to the manual.

The first step in quality planning means evaluating resources on hand and ensuring that resources are kept available for the right opportunities. Successful business people keep "dry powder" in reserve for unusually profitable opportunities. In your planning process, work hard to create working capital within the firm, to have lines of credit established and to have the people resources available for the best opportunities. I have found that when markets are moving downward and others are having difficulty, such times can represent the best opportunities for investment. But the only way to seize on such "anomalies of opportunity" is to have resources in reserve that can be deployed to capture great assets during stressed times. In 2005, it became apparent to me that investors were paying substantially higher multiples for office buildings in the Houston market—well above anything I had seen in the previous 20 years. So our firm began selling off our office portfolio, with the last sale occurring in late 2007, just as the financial markets were collapsing. In fact, our last two office buildings may have been the last office buildings to sell in Houston during that particular cycle.

During the downturn, I thought that prices for office buildings would erode and we would be able to begin replacing our office building portfolio in a few years. But instead, something else happened: the institutional buyers kept buying office buildings due to the need for yield. As interest rates continued their decline, the larger funds continued to buy office buildings and other income properties, which caused prices to remain relatively high. I believe, based on research I did while in graduate school, that the most successful investors have always been "value" buyers. Value buyers simply determine an asset's value and seek to acquire assets that are priced below the value investor's determined value. Our firm follows the value approach and therefore works hard to make what we feel are below-market acquisitions that represent value acquisitions. As the financial markets dried up and loans became very scarce between 2008 and 2011, the most distressed asset in Texas became land. Since loans were not available for land (as there is, in general, no yield received from land investments, thereby making land more challenging to finance) and investors were seeking yield type real estate, land prices dropped substantially. Fortunately, we had a number of longtime investor partners who not only trusted our judgment but also had strong, liquid capital positions. In 2009, we began buying land in and around Houston and continued to do so through 2013. It appears the investment in land assets will be a good decision, as land prices moved up rapidly as the development business in Houston became very active. Planning, coupled with keeping dry powder in store, can lead to attractive results. Like a pilot with a power reserve available for climb if necessary, so is an organization and its leadership team that has ample cash ready for deployment for unusual opportunities.

The second step to good planning is becoming an excellent evaluator of the current environment and future conditions that will exist during the plan's execution. Pilots are required to use both the airplane operating manual and the most current weather conditions report as part of their normal course of flying. Similarly, a good leader learns to continually check the organization's resources and evaluate external conditions. Like a good pilot who studies weather patterns and possible changes in forecast conditions, a strong leader becomes a student both of the economy and their particular industry. In my experience, the best business leaders are those with an innate sense of where the economy is headed and how their particular industry may fare in any given economic climate. One of the things we do in our company to develop a mindset for forecasting is to make regular one-dollar bets on probability. It is a game we play almost every day to make predictions about the future. I encourage this game because I want our team members to think about the future and to grade themselves on their forecasts. Losing one dollar may not have any real economic impact to the individuals making the wager, but there is a pride in wanting to be right. For most issues, as in an economic market, there is a counter party on our leadership team who will take the opposite view. For example, someone might say that a particular project might cost around X dollars, and I might say I will take the "under" on X dollars. Then one or more others on our leadership team will take the "over" or "under" on the issue. Now you may say that what I am promoting is gambling and I hope you see that the one-dollar wager is not much of a gamble, but a bit of "skin in the game" on one's opinion. We make a habit of paying off our wagers so that the pain of making a wrong guess is recorded both intellectually and emotionally. I have a number of signed dollars in my office as a reminder of being right on a particular opinion. Likewise, I have paid out a number of dollars to other leaders in our company when my opinion has been wrong—a good reminder that I missed on my forecast. The goal: learning to forecast better. Learning to develop a forecast and a plan is a key success factor for all leaders.

Like a pilot who chooses to fly purposely in a canyon, a leader who hopes to achieve the desired objective should have plans with contingency options that allow for flexibility in achieving the desired outcome. Leading an organization without written plans is paramount to flying a plane into a canyon hoping that the canyon has an exit path and is not a box canyon with no way out.

Chapter 6

Seeking Wise Counsel

While it is crucial for any leader to seek out wise counsel, it is equally important for that leader to accept the input and challenges of those he leads. In the following accident summary, it is apparent the pilot could have achieved a better outcome had he been able to hear the opinions of others.

About an hour after midnight, Korean Air Flight 801 from Seoul to Agana, Guam, radioed to the control tower in Guam. The plane was at 41,000 feet and 240 nautical miles out, and the controller cleared the flight to descend to 26,000 feet at the pilot's proceeding.

After briefing the approach to the controller, the captain complained about his exhaustive work hours and commented that he was sleepy. Shortly thereafter, his first officer noted that the conditions at Guam were "not good," and the flight faced significant cloud buildups, so he requested alternate deviations from the controller.

It should be noted that the glide slope, a ground-based navigational signal used by the plane's avionics to guide the plane to the runway, was not functional. Though the automated weather reported seven miles of visibility, the conditions at the terminal called for occasional heavy rain showers, which had reduced visibility.

The recorded final minutes from the Cockpit Voice Recorder revealed that the plane had crashed into high terrain 3.3 miles from the runway, and only several football fields away from the Nimitz VOR, the radio navigation signal for the terminal at Guam. Twenty-six passengers survived, but 228 (including the flight crew) did not.

Oddly, despite knowing during the pre-flight briefing that the glide slope was not operational, the captain discusses the glide slope in depth several times during the last three minutes of the flight.

With the glide slope not functional, the pilots were using a non-precision approach that required the airplane to "stepdown" in altitude at prescribed points ("fixes") along the approach. During Flight 801's approach, the captain loses clarity on where the plane is relative to the fixes and repeatedly called for the first officer to reset the altitude alerting system to the next fix prior to the plane reaching the previous fix. In other words, the captain and crew thought the plane was farther along the approach than was reality. Thus the airplane's altitude was prematurely reduced putting the airplane at too low of an altitude for the area terrain. As a result, the plane descended to its final altitude well before reaching the final approach fix, Nimitz VOR, which is the point at which the plane should have started its descent to the final approach altitude. Thus the plane was at final approach altitude miles earlier than is allowed by the approach causing the plane to fly directly into the terrain where the Nimitz VOR ground station was located. At no point did the crew members suggest alternate solutions for the captain to consider or suggest discontinuing the approach.

The National Transportation Safety Board determined two causes for the captain's confusion and the resulting accident: first, the captain's exhaustion, and second, the need for a change from an expected visual approach to an instrument approach due to the weather conditions. And although the pilot was approaching using the stepdown fixes depicted by the approach, he was doing so at the wrong intervals.

Although the captain had flown into Guam a month earlier and several times in a different aircraft some years prior, he may never have had to execute a landing with complete dependence on only the approach chart.

In a footnote, the Board identifies that "especially in high stress and workload situations...people...tend to ignore evidence that does not support an initial decision." Or, to put it another way, in some situations pilots may make up their minds and not be able to make a different decision despite evidence to the contrary.

The Korean Airlines accident highlights both the importance of good communication and also the need for corrective feedback. The leader must be willing and able to hear the opinions of others if he is to avoid crashing the organization into the rocks. Accordingly, those who are following a leader must be empowered to provide feedback and voice concerns. The leader of a group should hear concerns from those he is called to lead, even if he chooses other options than those presented by his followers.

As I mentioned earlier, the wise leader has wise counsel. The more critical the decision, the more important it is for the leader to search out the opinions of others. I have no doubt the decision to make the flight on that Thanksgiving holiday in east Texas would have been significantly different had I called one of my old flight instructors or pilot friends who had far more hours of flying time. Why did I not take the time to make such a call? In hindsight I believe the underlying reason I did not make the call for another's opinion is the same reason that underlies most leaders' failure to gain qualified counsel—pride.

C.S. Lewis described pride as the "great sin"—the sin that leads to all other sins. The word "sin" literally means to miss the mark. When we as leaders fail to listen to others' opinions or seek out qualified perspectives, we set out on courses that not only can truly miss the mark, but also put those we lead and our organizations at risk.

In Proverbs, we are told that "pride comes before the fall." One of the reasons pride comes before the fall is that the prideful person is overly dependent on his own opinion and unable to hear the opinions of others. Now, I am not saying that the leader is exempt from making critical decisions, but it is necessary that leaders make those decisions based upon the integration of data from critical, credible sources. As a leader, take a minute and think about the last time you received feedback differing from your own opinion and made a decision to either take a new direction or perhaps scrap the original plan based on that feedback. If your answer is that you rarely change direction based upon the feedback of others, then I would suggest that the folks following you, starting with your family, should be wary of the decisions you may make on their behalf.

So how can we increase accountability and feedback obtained from others? I would recommend for those of you who are married that you agree with your spouse not to hide issues from one another. You may be thinking, "What does my spouse have to do with leading my business or organization?" I have found that most couples that have been married any substantial amount of time find that each has discernment that is important to the other. I always am amazed to hear of businesspeople who leave their spouses in the dark with regard to the on-goings of their business life. Not only is the practice very unhealthy for the marriage relationship, it also is a good way to miss critical feedback. My wife Susan always has a great gift of discernment and is an excellent reader of people, a gift that is far superior to mine. Where I may want to overlook small things about a person in order to move forward on a particular transaction, Susan many times will question if the person is someone we should be doing business with— do they share our values? Susan cares about me and she cares about our business. She understands the critical areas of our business and how important it is for us to have shared values with our partners and customers. To not hear her opinion would be foolish on my part, to say the least. I suspect the same is true for most of you reading this book— your spouse is an excellent resource. Is he or she underutilized? Could you get your spouse more engaged in the organization to utilize their God-given temperament as a significant aid to your decision making? If so, I think you will find the shared involvement is healthy not only for the business but also for your relationship.

Another key source for feedback is having mentors that care about you first as a person and second as a leader. I have been truly blessed in my life to have had a number of great coaches and mentors. My high school football coach, John Kallinger, was one of several coaches who poured into me first as a person and second as football player. Playing for Coach Kallinger, I learned the value of hard work and intensity along with the need to have fun along the way. Coach Kallinger cared for me and it showed in the way he pushed me. In college, my position coach, Paul "Cash" Register, was a huge influence. Coach Register taught me to dig deep and find the will to win and succeed even when I thought the ability to succeed was not within me. Coach Register would push his players to the maximum but, like Coach Kallinger, he made it clear just how much he cared for his players. I will never forget the times when Coach Register greeted me during a game with tears in his eyes as I came off Kyle Field at Texas A&M, so great was his joy in how I had played the series (or maybe he was crying about how bad it was). He showed me that it is okay for a man to be passionate and allow his emotions to play out in what he does. He taught me much of what it means to work hard and love one another as teammates. During college and even more significantly after college, Coach R.C. Slocum, a member of the Coaches' Hall of Fame and Texas A&M's winningest coach, became my friend and mentor. I have spent much time with R.C. over the past 20 years and he is a man gifted in wisdom. Some people have the gift of wisdom—a gift given by God. These people have an acute sense of knowing the right moves to make at the right time. R.C. has constantly led me down the path toward right decisions.

I also have been blessed by the wisdom passed on generationally: through my father and father-in-law, Bill Caldwell and Don Stallings, both who have passed into eternal life, were men who taught me about life, faith, business, friendship, grief and a host of other subjects. Even though my father, a Presbyterian minister, only had a short business career, I learned from him how to treat people, why it is best not to judge others, and how to bestow grace (unmerited favor) to the people around me. I never can recall my dad ever speaking poorly of another person or judging another individual—his is a great legacy and one that I fall short of at times. My father-in-law taught me much about business and also about how to treat people. He was a successful homebuilder and was known to be a tough but fair businessman. Don never put money ahead of relationships. He was an extraordinary designer and builder. I learned so much about how to evaluate plans and build quality homes with features that connected people. Most importantly, I once again learned through Don about how to treat people. His many nights of counsel for 30 years cannot be measured in terms of their impact on my life.

I've also had the benefit of many real estate investment partners over the years who have invested not only their financial resources, but also many have become close friends and advisors. Chuck Watson, a well-known energy executive, became a partner in our company and provided me the opportunity to see how a high-level executive managed a multitude of business ventures by leveraging himself well. One of my closest friends and longest-term investors, Ron Pugh, has been of invaluable help over the years. Ron has always had an amazing sense of timing in regards to the economy, combined with a desire to succeed. Like others in my life, Ron has always valued relationships highly and taught me the importance of doing business with people who have shared values. Ron has been an incredible friend that has influenced many, many decisions I have made in business and in life.

In addition, our company utilizes a business advisory board comprised of a number of former executives who provide expert counsel to our leadership team and to me as a CEO. Their experience and wisdom is critical to helping our team make good quality decisions. Jack Little and Rob McKey are both good friends who led oil companies (Shell Oil Company and Conoco) and have been kind to serve on our advisory board. Jack and Rob bring amazing, large company experience to our company. One of the members of our advisory board, Clois Smith, actually serves as our company chaplain as part of Marketplace Ministry. Clois' counsel and friendship have been invaluable to me during both good and challenging times.

Without mentors like these and others, it would have been all the more difficult to stay on the path toward good decision making. A strong leader realizes when he needs to call in counsel.

Finally, and most importantly for me, is having a relationship with God that allows Him to pour into my life and my mind. For some that are reading this book, you may decide to skip what I am writing in this portion, but I cannot overstate the value that God has played in my life. In fact, without Him, there would not be life worth living. The idea that we are simply the culmination of randomness flies in the face of creation's reality. If you are a pilot, like me, you have likely been impacted by the majesty of what you have seen while flying, such as flying in the late afternoon and weaving between towering white cloud formations with the sun nearing sunset. Or you may have flown over scenery below that, when viewed with the perspective of altitude, reveals the creativity of what is below in a way that no one on the ground can experience. In these moments, it is almost inconceivable to me that one can deny the existence of God. Instead, we should be called to worship His majesty by what He has created. It truly is one of the greatest benefits of flying to see God's creation from a perspective that very few ever have the opportunity to experience. What does this have to do with wisdom in decision making?

In the scriptures, Proverbs 9:10-11 says, "The fear of the Lord is the beginning of wisdom, and knowledge of the Holy One is understanding. For through wisdom your days will be many, and years will be added to your life. If you are wise, your wisdom will reward you; if you are a mocker, you alone will suffer."

The early followers of God knew that fearing God, which means to put Him above us as Creator and the one of absolute authority, is the start of making wise decisions. Further, the passage above states that through such wisdom our lives will be extended. Certainly in flying one can easily see the benefit of making wise decisions and how unwise, ego-fed decision making can lead to a shortened lifespan.

Finally the passage says that a mocker (one who denies the existence of God) will alone suffer. The mocker must suffer alone because this person has no hope in something other than this life. So when life goes wrong, which it always does, the mocker has nothing and no one to turn to other than the world, which has proven to be unreliable. Therefore the mocker suffers alone.

For me, part of understanding God's call on my life begins each morning on my knees in prayer in my office. I get down on my knees, not out of some religious teaching or requirement (you will note I am not a fan of man's religious attempts) but because such a position is a position of humility that acknowledges I am not in control. After a time of praying to God and listening to Him, I go to the Scriptures and read until God stops me on a particular part of His Word. I then write down in a daily journal what God spoke to me out of His Word for that day and I use that word as the "play" for the day, in the sense of a sports analogy. I have had a daily journal now for many years, which started when I attended the JH Ranch in California. JH is a guest ranch that focuses on parent/teen and husband/wife relationships. At JH, I learned the value of journaling God's work in my life. I cannot underestimate the benefit of journaling one's life journey and in particular making note of how God intercedes in your life. These daily reminders become spiritual waypoints that when reviewed are reminders of God's faithfulness and His plan for one's life. As my friend, Bruce Johnston, founder of JH Ranch, likes to say, "If the creator of the universe tells you something, you might just want to write it down." On a daily basis, I desire to hear from God and seek His counsel. I believe and have found true that there is no greater counsel than that of God.

All leaders benefit from having wise counsel—not some, but all. It is ego that is unable to hear the opinions of others, particularly if the other person is qualified to speak on the issue and has proven wisdom on the subject matter. Developing the mind to allow others to speak into our life is critical to long-term success. Taking this point one step further, I believe that the person who denies the existence of God will miss the counsel of the One most prepared to provide the most fruit and meaning from these limited days we have on earth. Jesus said in Matthew 6 to "seek first the kingdom of God, then all these things will be given to you." What Jesus was referring to were the earthly desires in a person's heart. Jesus says that if we seek Him first, then God will order the things of this world in a way that leads to true fulfillment. Great leadership starts with God and then considers the opinion of others in making decisions that will result in true organizational success.

Chapter 7

Humility and Inspections

At the top of the list for seeking counsel and help is finding successful people whom you respect for their character. You may be asking how to go about finding such people to be a mentor or who are willing to help. The answer may surprise you—humility. The opposite of pride is humility. Pride is an unattractive quality, while humility is not only attractive but desired. When I say "humility," I do not mean false humility that says in words and/or actions, "I am just an unworthy person, just a speck of dirt." To the contrary, true humility is learning to say, "I may not know the best way to handle this issue." True humility allows one to say, "I was wrong," and, "I am sorry for what I did/said." True humility allows you to kill a deal, to walk away, to admit the project was more than we were ready to handle. True humility says, "You go first." True humility allows you to go to very successful people you know and admire and say, "Bob, I have a problem and need some counsel. Would you be willing to listen to the issue and then provide a few thoughts on how you would handle it?" Such an approach shows genuine humility, and I can't think of a time when a person of character has turned down my request for help. Humility says, "I do not have to have all the answers, and, in fact, I need to work on having better questions so that the quality people with whom I spend my time can help me find the answers." Humility says, "I do not have to make this flight—cancelling may nick my pride but it is the best long-term decision." Humility stands opposite to E.G.O.— "Edging God Out."

Some of the best business decisions I have made are deals that I did *not* do. Over the years, I have been amazed that some of the deals I so desperately wanted to make but was unable to put together ended up being flops for the other party. I am reminded of one particular transaction where a trusted adviser full of character provided me with counsel that I will never forget. A number of years ago, our firm had a land tract we owned under contract to sell to an apartment developer. Only days after contracting the land for sale, we received a second offer that was for one million more than the contract we had just agreed to with the multi-family developer. I called my longtime friend and legal counsel, Ellis Tudzin, and asked him if we were, in fact, bound by the current contract. I will never forget the counsel from Ellis (a member of our advisory board). Ellis said that, in fact, we could probably find some legal reasons to terminate the contract. He then went on to say, "But Fred your reputation is worth much more than a million dollars." As soon as Ellis made that comment, I immediately was convicted by his truthful counsel. Ellis had helped change a very money-motivated perspective to doing the right thing. We had agreed to terms with the first buyer and we would honor the agreement regardless of any other offers. I am so thankful for the counsel Ellis provided and the fact we did not do some legal maneuvering to get out of the first agreement. I have many times remembered Ellis' counsel over the years when tempted for more but doing right says to take less.

A key component of humility in business, I believe, is learning to evaluate transactions with a critical eye. It is ego and pride that assume all will go exactly as *I* have planned. Such ego leaves no room for error, nor does it acknowledge the fact that we are not all-knowing and our decisions are not always right. I am a firm believer that downside risk needs to be evaluated properly before venturing into a new business transaction. Such due diligence literally means the buyer will be diligent in investigating the asset(s) before buying.

In flying, there is a very similar process—the "pre-flight" inspection. The pre-flight inspection is the process by which the pilot or co-pilot inspects the airplane to make sure the plane is ready for flight. In private aviation the pilot is required to carry the pilot operating manual during a pre-flight inspection to make sure that every step of the inspection is completed. Do pilots follow this rule? Not necessarily, as many pilots have inspected the same plane literally hundreds of times, so the pre-flight list is memorized. But for the pilot who has inspected the same plane hundreds of times, there is an inherent danger as the pilot expects that all will be okay. The desire to fly and achieve the mission can become the operative driver for the pilot doing the pre-flight. No one, particularly the pilot, wants to delay or cancel a flight or mission. Thus the pilot expectantly inspects the plane looking to ensure that everything is right. I believe this is the wrong attitude in flying and the wrong attitude in business, particularly when it comes to due diligence.

General Aviation News reported a story of a non-fatal accident that occurred when a commercial pilot failed to do a thorough pre-flight inspection on his Cessna 172G. The plane's engine failed upon takeoff, after which the Cessna flipped over and crashed into power lines, leaving both the pilot and his passenger injured. When the

NTSB inspected his aircraft after the crash, they found the engine had been starved for fuel due to significant amounts of dirt in the fuel tanks, the fuel strainer and the carburetor fuel screen. Had the pilot done a required fuel check by straining the fuel, he likely would have discovered the issue.

The pilot in the above accident simply failed to do a basic pre-flight fuel inspection, which would have revealed the potential problem. The desire to go flying likely overtook the protocol that would have saved the pilot and passenger from serious injury. In flying, the accomplished pilot learns to inspect the airplane with a critical eye. He or she has trained the mind to look both for what is right and, more importantly, what may be wrong. The drip of oil on the hangar floor, the low air pressure in a tire, the low oil level that suggests adding another quart even though time is critical, or the nick in the propeller that is a bit larger than allowed tolerances are examples of issues that can turn into larger challenges in flying. The trained eye looks for small things that may point to larger problems. Most importantly, the pilot uses a pre-flight checklist to make sure that every recommended item is inspected. In your business, do you have a pre-purchase inspection list before hiring, buying equipment or acquiring an investment asset?

Likewise, the accomplished business leader does a critical review of assets being considered, both for acquisition (same applies to hiring processes) and with the mindset of why the acquisition should not be made. What could go wrong? What is the cost of holding the asset under worst-case assumptions? Why would this person not work out if you made the hire? I have found that in almost all hiring processes, there is a sense that top candidates will all add value. I also think a key issue is to consider before hiring how the person might not work out. An advantage of using the DISC or other similar assessment is finding those areas needing improvement, based on a candidate's temperament. I have found consistently that those particular areas identified by DISC have been issues for job applicants in their former jobs. Asking candidates tough questions about their previous jobs, including specific examples, provides more value than only looking for their good qualities. I have always considered a multiple interview hiring process to be the best process. If a candidate cannot survive several rounds of interviews, how will they do in our business when the pressure is on them to perform?

Similarly, I have found that most every asset acquisition has a built-in inertia, and the various consultants who are paid fees for putting deals together are great at keeping the momentum going to encourage the parties to make a deal. The strong leader and investor can put aside the desires of others and critically evaluate the asset by deploying a precise process, like a good pre-flight inspection, designed to find every anomaly. Do brokers and bankers hate a good due diligence process? Many times they do because they are afraid of losing the fees that will result from the transaction. The reality is that good due diligence will make you more successful and, over the long term, the consultants will make more on your account due to your success in making good buys.

Chapter 8

Faith

Now for some of you reading this book, you may be tempted to shut the cover at this juncture as you reach this chapter—such may be your internal reaction to the word "faith." You may already be frustrated by my references to God and the role of faith in my life. That is okay. I encourage you to hang with me for a bit longer and hear why I believe faith is a critical part of being an effective leader. If this isn't of help to you, you can discount the issue, but I suspect for many of you, faith may be a catalyst that opens your mind to a new way of thinking and living life.

In speaking about faith, make no mistake that I am not speaking about religion. To me the two are worlds apart and uniquely different. Let me explain. Religion is created by man and generally desired to please an envisioned angry God. When I hear people speak about religion, it is usually tied to a building or the way in which a person acts (I often hear people speak about someone they view as spiritual by saying "they are a very religious person"). Religion, when used in the context of our culture, is often used to describe a particular denomination or group of people and the way they choose to meet/act/live out their beliefs. The Methodists meet on Sunday morning at 10 a.m., the Baptists meet Wednesday night at 7 p.m. and on Sundays have several services. The Catholics meet on Saturday night or Sunday at a mass. The Jewish people meet on Saturdays in a synagogue or temple. And the list goes on describing people groups for the way those groups act toward God, and such is described as "religion."

"Faith," on the other hand, in the way I use the word, is something very personal and very relational. I choose to tell people regularly that I am not very religious. Some are taken by this comment since such people hear me speak openly about God and my faith. What I mean by the comment is I have no desire to repeat an activity over and over in the hopes of pleasing God—the root of man-made religion. Nor do I have a desire to act in a certain way simply to fit into an accepted religious process that pleases only man. Rather, my faith is placed in a personal relationship with God that says I can trust Him and He will do what is best for me because he loves me. Religions of the world say we will do things for God to appease Him because He is angry with me. One is based on love and one is based on fear. One is based on living out what God is doing in one's life, and the other is based on doing what has been taught as the religious order in the hope that God will be pleased. The difference is, in my opinion, not only eternally significant, but of utmost importance in daily decision making. The faithful person operates not out of fear or the need to measure up to cultural expectations but out of a belief in God's love and acceptance. The faithful person has the ultimate adviser in God whom they can access 24/7, an adviser who will always be with you as you build and create your legacy. But no matter how important your role/business may seem, ultimately your business and your role in the business will go away. One only needs to examine the annals of history to see that business legacies are short-lived at best. No, your true legacy will be built through your spouse, through your children and through the generations of descendants that will follow you. The question is not what your business associates will say about you when you die, but what your spouse, your children, you grandchildren and other loved ones will say. How were their lives impacted by your existence on earth? If you measured your investment in the business versus your family, how do the investment amounts compare? I mean no guilt trip here, just a reminder to love your family well. It has been my experience that loving my family well starts with me loving God. His love for us makes us into better leaders both in our families *and* our businesses. Coming to that understanding might just be the end of religion for some of you and the beginning of life. In the Bible, Jesus says in John 10:10 that He came to "give us life and give it to the full." I believe that statement as I have seen His life expand in my own. I hope this might be true for some of you reading this book—perhaps for the first time you will make God first in your life.

Chapter 9

Training and Speed

Throughout our careers, each of us will come to a point when we believe we know more than those professionals who have come before us. We believe that we have earned the right to ignore advice and forge ahead. But it is the experienced pilot and leader who, with humility, examines the situation, swallows his pride and takes a step back. In business, this is essential. In flying, it is critical, especially when the pilot hears the phrase: VFR (reference by sight versus flying by instruments) flight not recommended. Please consider the following accident as an example of the need for training.

Though this pilot had only 350 hours under his belt and was non-instrument-rated, he took off in his Cessna 150, embarking on a 125 nautical mile route through the states of Pennsylvania, Maryland and Virginia. Prior to the flight, the Altoona Flight Service informed him that VFR flight was not recommended, due to mountainous terrain and anticipated conditions that would call for instrument flight.

The Airman's Information Manual explains the "VFR not recommended" warning more specifically:

> *When VFR flight is proposed and sky conditions or visibilities are present or forecast, surface or aloft, that in the briefer's judgment would*

make flight under visual flight rules doubtful, the briefer will describe the conditions, affected locations, and use the phrase 'VFR flight is not recommended.' This recommendation is advisory in nature. The final decision as to whether the flight can be conducted safely rests solely with the pilot.

The airplane crashed almost vertically into a pasture near Bittinger, Maryland, just 30 miles from the starting point. The conditions included a very low overcast, with fog, drizzle and freezing rain. The crash site was on a direct path from Connellsville to Warrenton, leading investigators to conclude (and then confirm) that the pilot had a GPS aboard.

There is no clear reason for the pilot's beeline rush or his dismissal of the "VFR not recommended" warning. Forty nautical miles north, the gap at Johnstown would have given him a safe way through the mountains and below the overcast—though no doubt adding extra time to his trip. However, even without a briefer warning, it typically is very clear when VFR flight should not be attempted.

Another example of a VFR pilot attempting to fly in instrument conditions is described in the following accident summary. The Montana pilot of a Mooney M20F departed the Havre, Montana airport for his ranch strip 140 nautical miles to the southeast. While conditions at Havre were outstanding, they looked dismal off in the distance, and the pilot admitted that "it looked bad enough that he was not sure how far he would be able to get." An official briefing (which he did not obtain) would have absolutely warned him against VFR flight.

A witness saw the pilot approximately 15 minutes after takeoff, flying so low that the pilot could be seen inside the aircraft. The pilot and observer even waved to each other. Not long after, the pilot was dead and his airplane engulfed in flames.

He had struck a hundred-foot tree at 60 feet above ground, and the plane tore to pieces as it shredded other trees growing on an upward slope of the Little Rocky Mountains. Due to drizzle and snow showers, visibility in that area was under a mile. His intended destination bore the same conditions, only made worse by thick layers of ground fog.

As noted in the above accidents, VFR (visual flight rules) flight into known IFR (instrument flight rules, meaning to fly by instruments in the plane versus visual reference) conditions by pilots not trained (qualified) to fly in instrument conditions has proven to be a perfect recipe for a fatal crash. The reasons for pilots choosing to fly in instrument conditions when not qualified can vary, but the predominant theme centers on the "need" to get someplace, and the pilot rationalizes they can accomplish the mission in marginal VFR weather. When the weather turns out worse than hoped, the pilot ends up in instrument conditions without the proper training.

I can attest to the anxiety that arises in a pilot without an IFR rating when the weather starts to deteriorate. I recall flying to meet (ironically) my instrument flight instructor in Huntsville, Texas for one of my instrument training flights. The weather conditions were marginal VFR and below my comfort level, but the IFR instructor was persuasive about me making the flight so we could proceed with the lesson. I should have deferred the flight but my desire to complete the lesson and the voice of someone with far more hours than I had at the time caused me to get in the airplane and make the flight. The visibility for that flight was in fact marginal but still VFR and did not deteriorate, so the instructor was correct in telling me the flight would not be an issue. However, my personal risk meter told me not to make the flight, and I ignored the warning sign. Success in the one flight could in turn have led to other similar flights had I not obtained an instrument rating. One of the proven factors in pilots who push the envelope on safety is, many times, a previous history of other flights that pushed the envelope in the same area, yet ended satisfactorily— mission accomplished. In essence, success with poor technique can lead to continued missions with improper training and qualifications based on some previous success. Such decision making can be fatal in flying and disastrous for a company or other organization that is being led by an ego-driven leader who feels his lack of experience and training are no issue given past business success.

Training is a primary factor for a leader to consider after evaluating his own personal temperament and risk tolerance. Many organizations, particularly those led by entrepreneurs, are not great at training. I say this from the experience of having evaluated my own futility in training people. Yet I highly value training even though I am not the best person to develop or implement training programs.

From flying, I know that training is a critical component to safety and a primary factor in why the commercial aviation industry is able to complete missions throughout the world with a remarkable low loss of life per hour flown. The fact is, both the FAA and commercial airlines require substantial training and flight testing. For a person to become a private pilot, the minimum hours required before a person can legally fly the plane with passengers is 40 hours. Of the 40 hours, 20 must be dual time with an instructor and the remaining 20 are required to be solo. Of the 20 solo hours, the student pilot is required to fly three cross-country flights, a night flight and perform to other minimum standards. The reality is, the average flight time for student pilots is closer to 60 hours before their instructor will release the student pilot to take an FAA flight test administered by an FAA flight examiner. Should the student pilot not pass the test, the pilot will be called upon to do more work and then retake the flight test. Along the way, the student pilot also would have had to complete a written "ground" test demonstrating they understand the basics of major flying issues. The reality is that after obtaining a pilot's certificate, the pilot has only begun to learn and is not really qualified for any significant mission. The pilot needs to gain time and experience. The experience factor cannot be taught, but once a pilot has experience then he can add an instrument rating allowing for flight into instrument conditions as well as a number of other certificates and training, such as twin engine training, high performance airplane ratings and all the way up to a commercial license.

Now let's compare the requirements to become a pilot to the requirements to take the helm of a company or organization. For this example, let's take the typical 50- to 300-person company. Bob is Mary's friend and gets a job working in her business unit. Everyone in the unit likes Bob, and the CEO of the company has gotten to know Bob and sees that Bob is good with people. Furthermore, Bob is a good salesman and has helped bring in several new large accounts. Bob has proven he is a productive associate and after eighteen months appears to be ready for advancement. It just so happens that the CEO has a new business unit he desires to start and suggests to Mary that Bob run the unit. Mary, although disappointed to lose Bob from her team, is glad to see her friend Bob advance and gladly agrees that Bob would be an excellent fit. Bob is asked by the CEO to head the new unit, which, incidentally, is in a new product line that the company has never handled. Additionally, the new line has required a significant financial commitment by the company, and therefore the CEO will work directly with Bob to ensure that the new unit gets off to a good start. The CEO, being a high-D, entrepreneurial leader, can see no reason this new unit will not do great and, with his help, Bob will be an outstanding business unit leader.

Sound familiar? Sure does to me—I have done exactly what is described above multiple times. And yes, a few times it has worked out fine, and other times it has been a complete disaster. What is missing? First and foremost is the lack of an organizational commitment to training and minimum leadership standards.

What is your firm's commitment to training and what are your minimum standards for leadership? If you are like me, I resisted these two issues for years, but through flying I have come to appreciate the value of experience and training. There simply is no substitute for experience or the impact that training can have when implemented as part of a process for leadership development.

Our C.A.O. and General Counsel, Brad Fishman, has a temperament different than mine. Brad is a much lower D but a high-I and S. Brad is great with details and is very well-liked throughout our organization. He is an outstanding leader. He also is an outstanding teacher. A number of years ago, I asked Brad to develop a training program for our new hires and our salespeople. The program, titled Caldwell University, is unique in our industry. The monthly training focuses on subject matter from sales to leadership to legal issues. Brad and the head of our brokerage company, Jim Black, recently took the training to a new level by having a week-long training session that involved each leader in our company acting as a teacher, with a test given to the class participants at the end of the week. The attendees had to pass the test to qualify for a great offsite event that Friday afternoon. Great leadership by Brad and Jim sharpened the sword for our rising leaders as well as the leaders that taught the subject matter.

But what do we do to sharpen our senior leaders? I have found in our industry that there are multiple organizations that provide certifications predicated upon applicants taking multiple courses and attending various conferences. These kinds of certificates are good and I believe important for our leaders. However, I believe we can do more in our company, and perhaps the same is true for you and your organization. One of the ways I am pushing training for our leaders is requiring (yes—accountability) each leader who reports to me to take a course each year. During the year-end review, I discuss with each person their previous year and then suggest an area I would like to see the person "sharpen the saw."

In private aviation, pilots are required to have a bi-annual flight review given by a certified FAA flight examiner. The bi-annual flight review requirement means a pilot must meet every two years with an FAA certified flight instructor to assess the pilot's competency. The flight review involves both some ground school and time flying. I always enjoy the bi-annual as it allows me to fly with a person who can provide valuable counsel on my flying skills and strategies. The examiner's goal is not to pass or fail the pilot, but to evaluate the pilot to ensure he is operating within an acceptable safety margin and then provide counsel on how to improve his flight skills.

At our company, I believe in offsite leadership retreats. I use these retreats to help our leadership team grow together and strengthen their skills, much like the bi-annual flight review. I typically will have a minimum of two such meetings each year. Each meeting focuses on a particular topic, like communication or integration of business units. We bring in a speaker that I believe will have the respect of our leadership team. The speaker may be a paid consultant or another CEO/leader who has insight that would be valuable to our team. The point is twofold: to provide an opportunity for our leadership team to gain from the wisdom of a seasoned leader and to give our leadership team time to break bread together, laugh, discuss the company and generally spend time away from cell phones and email. I have found this process highly valuable and in keeping with the bi-annual flight review.

A key part of our company's process for helping everyone on the team improve is what we call peer review. We are inconsistent in the application of this process but I have no doubt in its value. The peer review is a review form completed by one's peers grading the person on how well they are living up to our core values and achieving the unit's goals. Commonly known as a "360" review, the peer review provides each associate an accurate understanding of how others within the firm view their abilities.

In addition to peer reviews, our company uses quarterly reviews to provide regular feedback. I believe the annual review process is a horribly flawed process unless coupled with regular coaching. To have only one review each year is at best a way to meet some industry standard but, I believe, has little value for improving performance. A better process is a quarterly system of coaching that shapes behavior along the way. Such coaching sessions are designed to be more of a coaching/counseling session than a formal review. In the quarterly review, the leader and team member review the person's goals and discuss how they are doing in accomplishing their goals (business and personal—both are required). The conversation can be a great team-building exercise and way to help build confidence into the person while helping re-direct activity as may be necessary to help the person reach maximum performance.

Finally on the topic of training and accountability, what is the minimum recurrent training requirement for the CEO/organizational leader? What are *your* personal training standards? When did you last take a course on something relevant to your business? When did you last take a test—one that required you to think and really use your brain cells to answer the questions?

I ask these questions knowing that I fall short in this area myself. I am an avid reader but seldom take courses due, perhaps, to time constraints. But the reality is I would be a better leader if I made taking a course once per year part of my requirement for being the organizational leader.

I believe that most CEOs do not commit to ongoing training. There is not a review process or a board saying, "How are you doing in these specific areas?" But the reality is that we all need training to sharpen our skills, to stay current on the latest strategies and technologies and to help us stay away from—or escape—the trap that we are all susceptible to entering when we simply do the same thing day after day, year after year. The willingness to go through training is all about accountability. It's about discovering our weaknesses, as well as our strengths, so that we can improve the strengths or delegate weaknesses. It's about staying sharp and making a commitment—one that is seen by all of our employees—to continuing education and improvement. And it's about checking your ego at the door and accepting the fact that we all can improve in some areas.

I had a valued friend and CEO coach, Milton Schopper, who walked alongside me for about eight years. I gave him permission to critique me and I met with him every month during that time.

He pointed out things in my character and commented on my temperament, my God-given wiring and so forth. His feedback helped me immeasurably as a leader. In all of us, sometimes our strengths are also our weaknesses. He was able to sharpen my strengths and spotlight my weaknesses.

I also was a participant in a monthly CEO roundtable group for many years. We met to discuss issues, trends and lessons from each of our businesses. It provided great insight and it made us accountable to each other. We were all from different industries, but there is nothing like listening to another person's problems and to recognize that other people have the same issues and problems that you face. It was some of the most effective training I have received, and it made me a better leader.

Every time I have a bi-annual flight review, I learn something new. It always makes me a better and safer pilot. On a recent BFR, my trainer was a former commercial pilot with Continental, which made him the highest-level trainer who has ever reviewed me. He suggested that in the airport environment, I should consider turning on every exterior light. That's not an FAA requirement, but it makes great sense. A light bulb costs nothing, and one of the most dangerous places in aviation is near the airport. With heavy traffic and so many pilots talking to the tower, it just makes sense to illuminate your plane. It is not a requirement, but it was a great idea. After 700-plus hours of flying under my belt, I learned a great lesson that I added to my pre-flight checklist.

Similarly, having experienced advisers associated with your business can greatly aid your ability to make quality decisions. We are fortunate in our firm to have a very strong advisory board that consists of seasoned business executives who are willing to help coach and counsel our leadership team. We meet twice each year to listen to their suggestions and counsel on a host of issues, from personnel to strategic initiatives. I also take time to meet with the group in the absence of our leadership team to solicit thoughts on how I can improve as CEO. The comments and counsel cannot be overvalued. I would strongly encourage you to look at inviting other executives into your world to provide counsel—the benefits, I suspect, will be substantial.

A critical factor related to training is speed. I believe it is critical to plan the mission first but once the plan is determined, then it is time to move swiftly. For the past 17 years, our firm has had a very simple mission statement: "Doing It Right. Right Now." A consultant who worked with our firm long ago coined the slogan after evaluating our culture. After a short period of time, the consultant met with me to discuss what he believed were two primary values in the firm. The first was that we deeply cared about doing the right thing and second was that our teams had a very high sense of urgency. There was a need in our shop to get things done right now and not later. His comments lead to the genesis of our mission statement, "Doing It Right. Right Now," or as we say internally: "DIRRN." I have long thought that his assessment was correct and that the slogan should be our company's mission each day. To determine the right thing to do and then once determined, to act with urgency, is the foundation of our company's culture. It is often said that luck is where preparation and opportunity intersect. I have no belief in luck, but I have a strong belief in preparing to win and then executing swiftly upon each opportunity.

The high-D leader can have an advantage over other leadership temperaments when it comes to speed, in that the high-D temperament is wired perfectly for taking action. Once a plan is developed and the leadership team has mostly bought in, it is then time to move. I say "mostly" in regards to the leadership team because I have found that on a good leadership team there is a range of personalities and temperaments. A good leadership team will have those that are much more cautious than a high-D leader and may want to re-plan the mission or take more time to evaluate the environment. It is difficult to get all team members to reach consensus on all decisions, and it ultimately is the leader's decision on whether to launch. As a pilot ultimately must decide to take off, so a leader must decide whether to proceed with a particular plan.

In our development business, I am a huge fan of tearing up architect's plans until our team has a sense that we have the "right" design. Once we have settled on a design, I get very focused on execution. The design part of the process tends to be frustrating to my other high-D team members, but I have learned over the years that extensive planning on major development items makes for a better development. In addition, including a variety of participants in the design process helps to gather opinions but ultimately the design cannot be a matter of consensus; it must reflect the vision of the architect or team leader. I have seen many plans miss the mark due to the vision being "watered down" by too many others' ideas being incorporated into the design. Once the plan is determined, however, I turn on the jets and really rally the troops to execute. I do this by holding many meetings about the vision for the project and tend to over-communicate on the front end until I sense there is no lack of team buy-in or the importance of proceeding rapidly. I do believe that speed to market of a well-thought-out plan is an essential part of success. The famous Chinese General, Sun Tzu, made it clear that defeating an enemy can be successfully accomplished through rigorous planning then rapid execution. Sun Tzu knew firsthand, as one of the most successful military leaders in history, the value of well-planned speed. He is quoted as saying, "What is of the greatest importance in war is extraordinary speed: One cannot afford to neglect opportunity."

Chapter 10

Experience and Skills

I have mentioned experience multiple times but want to address the topic more specifically, particularly as it relates to flight. In flying, experience can be the difference between life and death, as was recently demonstrated in the crash of a Korean 777 at San Francisco airport. The NTSB findings cite, among other things, a failure by the pilots to manage the automated systems in the cockpit correctly. It appears that the co-pilot with low time in the 777 was hand-flying the airplane (not using the autopilot) on a steep approach over water. The runway's instrument landing system (ILS) was not operating, which meant the pilots would need to perform what is known as a visual approach. The proper approach slope to the runway known as the glide slope would need to be flown without the use of an autopilot. There is a growing concern in aviation that pilots, both in commercial and general aviation, are becoming too dependent on autopilots and cockpit automation, which is causing basic flying skills to erode as pilots rely more on button-pushing than "hand" flying. The NTSB report cites that the pilots became confused as to the use of the auto-throttles, and it appears the pilot in command ("PIC") realized way too late that the plane's sink rate was too high, which was exacerbated by his pulling the throttles to neutral. The steep approach and lack of thrust put the airplane in a dire position when the PIC realized too late that the plane was too low. The plane simply lacked timely power to restore the airplane to a climb before contacting the ground in a tail-low attitude. The relatively long time (compared to a prop-driven plane) for a jet engine to regain thrust (spool up) was simply too long for the pilot to establish a climb and get out of the nose-high/tail-low altitude the pilot had established on a steep descent.

Why is experience in a particular aircraft type important? The above tragic accident is a great example. The pilot flying the accident aircraft, while low in 777 time, was a 9,000-plus hour pilot—a high-time pilot and not a rookie. While it is easy to analyze what happened if you know something about flying, it is another thing completely to be in the cockpit and know what to do if faced with a similar situation. I have no clue how to even start a 777, much less what the sight picture should look like out the cockpit when doing a visual approach with a standard glide slope, or how long it might take for the engines to spool back up if behind the power curve. At some point, most all flying requires a sense of feel for the airplane and its attitude relative to the ground. You can fly modern airplanes by autopilot for the majority of the flight mission, but at certain critical points the pilot generally must take over from the autopilot (excluding highly advanced commercial airliners that have auto-land features) and hand-fly the plane. Hand-flying an airplane takes feel for the plane and an understanding of the systems. The feel for how an airplane flies in varying flight conditions is a function of time invested by the pilot and time is what leads to experience. Pilots who have substantial time in a particular airplane should supervise or train those who lack significant time in the aircraft type.

The same is true in leading an organization. The experience required to lead a single business unit enterprise with one product line is significantly different than the experience required to lead a multiple business unit company with multiple products. The experience and skills required to lead a public company are significantly different than the experience and skills required to lead a private company. As leaders, we have all failed in multiple areas of leadership. I have made more mistakes than would seem imaginable, yet by the grace of God our firm has survived. I even keep a notebook in which I take time at the end of each year to summarize, among other things, the errors I made in that particular year. Making mistakes is part of our human experience and is certainly part of the process we use for learning, from riding a bicycle to running a large public company. However, making mistakes is not always the best way to learn. In the case of the pilot error in the San Francisco crash, flying the actual plane was obviously not the best way to learn. Families will be forever impacted by the pilot's lack of experience and associated poor judgment. The same, to a much lesser degree, is true in our companies. Putting inexperienced leaders in charge of units or organizations with the hope they will succeed is a very risky strategy and generally should be avoided. The inexperienced leader should be mentored, trained and required to meet a set of standards before being given the controls.

Chapter 11

Communication: Why Words Matter

Good communication is the key to any successful flight or business transaction. Consider the following accident as you think about the importance of communication within a leadership team.

May 10, 2004 saw an accident that led to the deaths of two private pilots flying a Piper Seminole (N304PA). The pilots had crashed into mountainous terrain near Julian, California, while enroute from Deer Valley, Arizona, to Carlsbad, California. There were five company airplanes simultaneously flying the same route. One plane has a tail number of N304PA and was fourth in line, while a third airplane had the tail number of N434PA and flew directly in front of N304PA. When N304PA called the San Diego North Radar (SDNR), the craft reported level at 8,000 feet; the controller in the San Diego tower soon after cleared N434PA (the airplane preceding) to descend to 6,000 feet. The SDNR then instructed "Seminole four papa alpha" to descend to 5,200 feet, which the pilot of N304PA understood as his instructions and acknowledged accordingly. However, the SDNR's instructions actually had been for N434PA—the plane in front of the accident aircraft. It is important to note that the tail numbers for both planes end with "four papa alpha."

The tower cleared N434PA a second time to descend and maintain 5,200 feet. Not long after, the SDNR received a minimum safe altitude warning (MSAW) alert of N304PA, along with two other alerts. The controller did not act on any of these warnings.

N304PA disappeared out of radar coverage and crashed on a ridgeline just 200 yards south of the Julian VOR at an altitude of 5,537 feet. The NTSB declared the causes of the accident: an incorrect abbreviated call sign from the controller, the clearance for descent to N434PA, and the failure to recognize the incomplete confirmation from the pilot of N304PA. Lastly, the controller failed to act upon the warning alerts they received just prior to the accident. With the use of full call signs, as well as the pilot's better understanding of the terrain, the accident may have been avoided.

Communication is essential in flying and includes communication with air traffic controllers, ground controllers, airport tower controllers, co-pilots and passengers. When learning to fly, one of the most challenging items is learning to communicate in the manner required by the flying community. Not only is certain language and phraseology required, but the pilot also must be able to communicate in very brief statements while understanding similar controller statements that direct the pilot's actions. Pilots and air controllers utilize their own brand of language to ensure rapid, precise communication as frequencies are used simultaneously by many different pilots, all of whom may be handled by the same controller. Each pilot must be brief to allow the next communication to occur between the controller and other pilots. Most people cannot believe the speed of the communication and strange sounding phrases that occur between the pilots and the air controllers. The sound truly can seem like a foreign language, but over time (experience) the pilot learns to speak in the manner that is expected by the air controllers, and similarly, the pilot learns to hear without confusion what is being communicated. The pilot also learns to hear their tail number called even when the controller is speaking rapidly to multiple planes and calling a variety of tail numbers. An example communication would go something like: "November 65217 cleared direct Navasota VOR, maintain 3000." After which I would respond with: "Cleared direct Navasota VOR, maintain 3000, November 65217." The communication process is called "read-back phraseology" and creates a simple system for ensuring that commands are understood between pilot and the controller. Whatever commands the controller issues, the pilot repeats the command (reads back). The

Great communicators are great listeners.

pilot must respect the authority of the controller and trust that the controller knows what is best for all parties. Otherwise, chaos would reign in the skies.

How often in your organization is communication misinterpreted? How often do you think one thing was communicated but the listener heard something different—sometimes very different? We live in a multi-media world, and I am more and more convinced that the art of listening is a dying skill. Great communicators are great listeners. Flying requires the pilot to listen, for failure to listen to the controller can at best lead to a slap on the hand, and at worst, lead to suspension of the pilot's license or even a midair collision.

The risks in business may be lower, but quality communication is still a requisite skill for the successful leader. I believe the read-back process is a good process to employ in business, particularly when tensions and stakes are high. How does a leader deploy this with their team? The answer is fairly simple: when you hear a statement, confirm the statement either orally or via email/text. If you, the leader, start using a read-back communication style, I suspect that it will not be long before your reports will start mirroring your actions. How might this look? "Fred, can you take a look at this analysis on the new development project? We need to make a decision on the assumptions being used in the model and then present to the investment committee." I would respond then with something like: "Thanks for the analysis. I will review the assumptions and comment on any changes I think we should implement. What day is the investment committee meeting and by when do you need my comments?"

The process is really just basic, easy-to-implement communication. Commit to using this style of communication for 21 days and note how it improves your interaction with associates.

Chapter 12

Emotional Margin

There may come a point in flying—and in business—when the trip or deal simply needs to be aborted. When overwhelming factors cause us not to be in the right emotional or mental state, or it becomes obvious that the flight plan isn't going to work, it would be a good time to defer the mission. Such was the case in the flight that took the lives of John F. Kennedy, Jr. and two others.

The following is a brief overview of the Kennedy plane crash that occurred on July 16, 1999.

WEATHER

Kennedy had to contend with haze and limited visibility. The night of the crash, the weather was officially listed as VFR (Visual Flight Rules), which meant that Kennedy (who was not instrument rated) was legal to fly his plane. But visibility was poor in Essex County, New Jersey, with airports reporting between five and eight miles of haze and clouds. Marginal visibility can be disconcerting to a non-instrument rated pilot.

INEXPERIENCE

Kennedy was a relatively inexperienced pilot. He obtained his private pilot license in April 1998 and had received a "high performance airplane" endorsement in June 1998 along with a complex airplane endorsement two months before the crash. Kennedy's estimated total flight experience was about 310 hours, of which 55 hours were at night. His estimated experience flying his plane without a certified flight instructor (CFI) on board was only 72 hours. He had the relevant experience and the knowledge to make the flight under normal emotional circumstances but was clearly not a highly experienced pilot.

PILOT TRAINING

The CFI who prepared Kennedy for his private pilot check flight commented on two prevalent issues of Kennedy's flying (though the instructor did state that Kennedy had "very good" flying skills): the first, that he still required help with the rudder pedals due to an ankle injury that he suffered six weeks prior in a paragliding accident, the second, that he had difficulty flying without a visible horizon. The instructor also stated that the pilot was not ready for an instrument evaluation, and needed additional training.

PSYCHOLOGICAL STRESS

According to the Aeronautical Information Manual (AIM): "Stress from everyday living can impair pilot performance, often in subtle ways. Distractions can so interfere with judgment that unwarranted risks are taken, such as flying into deteriorating weather conditions to keep on schedule." Kennedy had spent the final three nights of his life away from his wife, and his magazine reportedly was having significant financial troubles.

PILOT DISTRACTION

Kennedy's plane flew into the path of American Airlines Flight 1484, which was on the approach to Westchester County Airport.

Controllers instructed the American Airlines jet to descend to avoid a collision. The two aircraft came "uncomfortably close."

No flight plan or request for help

Kennedy never received a weather briefing or filed a flight plan with any Flight Service Station. Except for the takeoff portion of his flight, Kennedy did not contact any air traffic controllers; during the flight, he never requested help or declared an emergency.

Late departure

The flight was originally scheduled for daylight hours, but had to be postponed after Kennedy's sister-in-law was delayed at work. Heavy traffic further delayed Kennedy's flight and pushed it back until after dark. Originally planned to depart at 6:00 p.m., the flight departed in a darkly lit sky at 8:39 p.m. instead, nearly thirty minutes past sunset.

Flight over featureless, open water

After passing Point Judith, Rhode Island, Kennedy's plane headed directly toward Martha's Vineyard, rather than following the Rhode Island coast, he chose a shorter, direct path over a 30-mile open stretch of water. According to the FAA Airplane Flying Handbook, crossing large bodies of water at night may be hazardous because the featureless horizon visually blends with the water, making depth perception and orientation difficult.

Wrong frequencies

When the National Transportation Safety Board (NTSB) examined the wreckage, it discovered that both of Kennedy's radios had incorrect frequencies selected, off by just slight amounts.

The NTSB was unable to determine whether or not these settings contributed to the crash.

The Kennedy accident gained much media attention, both because it was another tragic loss to the Kennedy family and also because his death was related to piloting a single-engine private plane. His accident has been the object of much scrutiny; speculation for the crash included everything from minimal hours as pilot in command (PIC)—that is, flying without an instructor in the adjacent seat—to distractions both in and outside of the cockpit. I have read much about the accident and it appears that Kennedy was a competent pilot even though he did lack many PIC hours (recall the accident summaries for pilots with under 300 total hours).

Much of the research suggests that his emotional state was a significant factor in the accident as it could have led to errors in the cockpit. It doesn't take much imagination to see that a budding, high-profile entrepreneur whose business and marriage were under high stress would be emotionally taxed. Couple those factors with an ankle injury and possible family distractions inside the cockpit, and anyone can see a dangerous scene unfold. I can imagine that despite whatever fears his passengers might have had about the flight, Kennedy was determined to prove he could pilot the plane successfully to Martha's Vineyard, even after his departure was delayed by the late arrival of his passengers. Would he have made the same decision if he hadn't been under such stress?

In flying, as in business, a leader who has a questionable emotional state can and will make poor decisions. Why do we allow ourselves to end up in such poor mental states?

The leader has to do it all—run the company, make the meetings, attend the fundraisers, be an example, answer 300 emails a day, spend quality time with spouse and family—the list goes on and on. The reality is that it is impossible to balance all the demands on our time without causing grief somewhere. Oftentimes, that grief translates into stress—stress that demands to be medicated in some way or other, including alcohol. Stress can cause many to withdraw and, in some cases, exhibit much anger. The question becomes how to deploy strategies that help us make better decisions in high-demand jobs and increase margin (non-committed time) in our lives?

A flying acronym that offers rules for dealing with a pilot's emotional state and ability to make a particular flight can be helpful in evaluating your own state of mind and ability to perform at the highest level. Consider the "I'M SAFE" flying acronym used by pilots to assess their readiness to fly an airplane:

I—Illness. Are you ill and unable to make the flight? Similarly, illness affects our ability to make quality decisions as leaders. Staying in good physical health is essential to being a quality leader. Exercise is a great way to battle stress. A twenty-minute workout on a stationary bike or vigorous walk can do wonders for my mental state as endorphins kick off in my brain and eliminate stress with each bead of sweat. If you are in bad physical shape and called to lead others, you are not doing your best for those you are called to lead. Lack of time is not an excuse (I used this myself for a long time before reality set in), as dying of a heart attack or stroke will not provide you with more time.

M—Medication. Are you ill and taking drugs that impair your decision making? Many drugs are regulated by the FAA and prohibited from being taken while acting as pilot in command. Over-the-counter painkillers and cold medicines, along with a variety of prescription drugs, can significantly affect mental acuity and ability to make quality decisions. I am rarely ill but when I do feel sick, I make it a point to avoid major decisions. When thinking about decisions made while under the influence of medications, consider the following accident.

In late spring of 2001, a 38-year old private pilot entered a flying club in Reno, Nevada, where he was checked out a Piper Warrior plane. The flight instructor reminded him that the plane was not capable of carrying four adults due to limited weight carrying ability. The instructor also told the pilot that five hours of local flying time were required before a member could use a plane for a cross-country flight.

Though the pilot booked the plane for most of Tuesday and all day Wednesday, supposedly to complete the mandatory five hours, those were never completed. At 4:30 a.m., he had obtained a weather briefing for Reno to Denver, and he filed a VFR flight plan to the airport at Hawthorne, Nevada that same morning. Right away, upon takeoff, another pilot saw the Warrior struggling for altitude along its flight path. The pilot had only added 20 gallons of fuel for the 130 nautical mile flight to Jeffco—in part, no doubt, because of the three other adults he had brought along as passengers.

The four people in the plane were headed for the Stanley Cup in Denver but never arrived. Six days after departure, debris that had been discovered by local fishermen were identified as part of the missing aircraft. A further search revealed and recovered the airplane's wreckage from 43 feet of water. The front seat passengers had died of impact-related injuries, while the two back seat occupants had drowned. As the investigation continued, officials concluded that nothing appeared to be wrong with the engine.

The pilot had no prior experience in this type of aircraft, and his total flying time was only 282.7 hours—of which few hours had been completed recently. By going against the flight instructor's orders, he deliberately failed to exercise prudence or caution.

When the FAA's Civil Aeromedical Institute performed a toxicological screen on the pilot's body, they found methamphetamine in both his blood and urine. The levels implied regular use, even addiction; it was more than likely that he had recently used the drug and was hindered by its effect. The official probable cause was "the pilot's failure to maintain terrain clearance as a result of his drug-induced impairment."

Drugs and flying are clearly a bad combination. The pilot in the above accident made terrible decisions because the drugs in his system made it impossible to process information properly. The FAA regulates drugs of all types, including common cold medicines, due to their impact on decision making. As a leader, be careful making significant business decisions when you are under the influence of mind-altering drugs (which include even common cold medicines). Defer the decision, get well, get off the drugs and make a clear-headed plan for moving forward.

Remind yourself to stay "SAFE" by avoiding the following:

S—Stress. Stress is a killer, literally. Too much stress causes the body to shut down. People who seem to be in great physical shape still succumb to heart attacks, strokes and other chronic illnesses due to the impact of stress. Interestingly, too little stress can lead to equally bad issues and is a leading cause of alcoholism among retirees. I am not a big fan of the retirement concept, and lack of stress is a good reason to avoid the idea of retirement. Rather, a better concept may be to think about "new chapters in life" that lead to continued learning, experience and fulfillment as you leverage your God-given abilities. Both ends of the spectrum—too much stress or too little—wreak havoc on your emotional state. If you have too much stress, you need to offload responsibilities until you return to normal emotional health. Likewise, if you don't have enough stress due to underutilization of your mind, you need to add activities that will force your mind to work again.

A—Alcohol. Drinking and driving is a leading cause of traffic accidents. Drinking and flying is a worse combination. The FAA requires a minimum of 8 hours between the last drink and being legal to act as pilot in command ("8 hours bottle to throttle"). Obviously, other drugs are as bad or worse and cannot be tolerated in a flight environment. The ability to make quality decisions is significantly impaired by alcohol and drugs. Yet, I am amazed to see executives go knock down a number of drinks with other executives, all in the name of cutting a deal. I know many deals have been done by executives in bars, but find it true folly in the long run. The impact of alcohol on the brain is well-documented, causing decision making to decrease significantly with increasing consumption of alcohol. I know, without reservation, the worst decisions I have made in my life have been while under the influence of alcohol. If you have major decisions to make about your organization, wait to make those decisions until your mind is clear.

I worked for a man early in my career who never made a significant business decision late in the day, much less while consuming alcohol. Mr. Ben Reynolds Jr., an important mentor in my life, would simply tell anyone asking for him to make an important decision late in the day, "Let me sleep on it and I will get back to you tomorrow." Such an answer gives you time to think and defer a decision you might later regret.

F—Fatigue. One expert forecasted that the personal computer would be the invention that would cut our work week in half and, in fact, we would not know what to do with all the extra time. Talk about a miscalculation! Wow. The amount of data and information that flows through the typical executive's computer and cell phone today is almost beyond comprehension. The demands of running a business or other organization coupled with family and other commitments often moves a leader to the point of exhaustion. To combat exhaustion over the years, I have found two key disciplines: regular exercise and a commitment to take time off. For many years, I would only take a few days off at a time. I took my first 10-day vacation about three years ago, after 27 years of business. I made a discovery: I did not sleep well for a week. After seven days away from the office, I found a new pace and relaxed state that came from reduced stress. I now commit to taking two weeks off in sequence each year, in addition to other short excursions.

The reality is our bodies and minds are not designed to run for months on end with overload. We should rest. The 23rd Psalm reminds us, "The Lord is my Shepherd. I shall not be in want. He makes me lie down in green pastures. He restores my soul." God desires that we rest. He desires to restore our souls. If we do not rest, He can make us lie down. Ego drives many executives to unhealthy lifestyles including chronic states of fatigue. The reality is that these driven individuals are many times simply playing out the wounding experienced in childhood by a parent or other adult. Many times the unmet expectations of a parent play out in the child's adult life in unhealthy ways. It is another subject, but if you struggle with feeling guilty for taking time off, check deep inside why that guilt exists. If you are like me, it may be rooted in growing up in a performance-based environment. Let go of it—there is a better way.

E—Eating (and Hydration). Nutrition may seem like a silly subject to include in a book on leadership, but we are physical creatures, and taking care of our bodies is a critical part of our existence on Earth. Like exercise, proper nutrition is important for making quality decisions. In flying and in decision making, one of the key factors for success is ensuring that our bodies are hydrated. Studies have shown that our bodies dehydrate significantly overnight while we sleep. One of the best things we can do to improve performance is to start the day with a large glass of water or a water bottle. Each morning, I drink a full water bottle during my quiet time. Only later will I have a cup of coffee. The first thing I want to do is hydrate my body after sleep, which studies have shown, improves the ability of the brain to process information. In flying, particularly on long cross-country trips, it is wise to carry a couple water bottles so that the body can remain hydrated and the mind will remain sharp. Similarly, drinking water through the workday is far superior to drinking coffee or soft drinks filled with caffeine. What we eat is also critical. In an age when diets range from A to Z in terms of what to eat, I believe the Biblical command of moderation applies also to food. To go too far in any particular direction with our eating habits seems to me a bit foolish. The long-time science seems to support balanced meals—protein, vegetables and carbohydrates that all work well together.

Chapter 13

Vision

CFIT is an aviation term for controlled flight into terrain, an incident where an aircraft is unintentionally flown into the ground, water or another similar obstacle. The term only applies when the airplane in question was otherwise controllable (undamaged at the time of the incident). CFIT is a leading cause of fatal crashes around the globe, particularly in the case of older aircraft without the latest generation glass cockpits. So it is a bit unusual when an experienced airline crew flying in a highly sophisticated glass cockpit experiences a CFIT crash as the following accident summary describes.

A Boeing 757—a U.S. carrier—impacted a mountainside near Cali, Columbia, on December 20, 1995 in an unusual set of events given the modern aircraft and knowledgeable flight personnel. American Airlines Flight 965 (AA965) had an experienced pilot, a seasoned crew and a cutting-edge flight management system (FMS). Flight AA965 left Miami at 6:35 p.m., and just under three hours later, requested the controller clear the flight to descend on Runway 1 in the Cali airfield. Instead, the controller offered a much shorter approach into Runway 19, putting the aircraft at a significantly high altitude.

The captain immediately requested a lower altitude, for which the controller cleared AA965. At 9:37 p.m., after passing the Tulua VOR, the plane began to fly east, but for only a minute. Flight transcripts indicate confusion on behalf of the first officer, as he asked the captain, "Uh, where are we...where [are] we headed?" The captain's response? "I don't know...what happened here?"

Just minutes later, the aircraft radioed in to confirm the plane's approach to Runway 19. At 9:40 p.m., the captain confirmed an altitude of ten thousand feet, and just a minute later, down to nine thousand. At 9:41 p.m., the ground proximity warning system (GPWS) alerted the plane to terrain close ahead. Despite efforts by the captain and crew to add power and climb, at 9:42 p.m., Flight AA965 crashed into El Deluvio Mountain at nearly 9,000 feet, 28 miles north of Runway 19. Only four passengers survived out of 155, and the entire flight and cabin crew was lost.

Investigators found no mechanical failure in the aircraft or its systems. Weather had not factored into the crash, the navigation system was fully functional and the crew had adequate qualifications. But the pilot, who was making a routine trip to a familiar airport, fell into complacency, failing to make the effort to clarify with the controller (a native Spanish speaker giving instruction in English) the course change. Simply put, the crew lost situational awareness when the controller switched the plane to a new runway. The new runway destination required a different approach process. The crew did not revise its plan fast enough for the controllers' change in runways. Nor was the crew's internal communication good, as the first officer never bothered to challenge the decision to continue, and the captain made no effort to start the approach over when it was apparent that the airliner was not on course. The Cali, Columbia, accident clearly highlights the need to gain clarity of situation when not sure of position before proceeding. The same is true for us in life and in business. There are times when it is best to simply gain altitude and hold until we have clear vision on how to proceed.

In flying, there are times when we simply enjoy taking to the skies for a joyride. We can take family members or friends on a fun flight to give them a new perspective. We don't need an agenda, a flight plan or a destination location. We have no trip purpose in making that type of flight other than having fun, seeing some of the sights below and enjoying God's creation. But when I want the airplane to become a useful business tool, I must have a clear vision of where I want to go. If I am in Houston and I need to go to Tyler for a meeting, I have a clear vision of where I want to go. I can view various maps online to see what the routing will be. I can establish checkpoints along the way and can establish clear coordinates to keep me on my path. Even with many hours of experience in the cockpit, most pilots would never get into the cockpit and fly to Amarillo, Austin or Albuquerque without filing a flight plan with the FAA.

There is a significant amount of planning and mapping for every flight, no matter if it is a quick flight from Houston to College Station or a much longer one. I monitor location and altitude checkpoints to ensure that I am on track to my destination and that I am not wasting time or fuel by not following the most direct route. And if I discover I am off-track, that feedback will immediately allow me to reroute. Obviously, this is extremely rudimentary information for pilots. But so many of us as CEOs fail to take the same approach to how we run our businesses on a day-to-day basis.

In many organizations, there is a lack of goal clarity. Like Flight 965 in the above accident, many organizations and leaders fail to have clarity on their current location and the proper next waypoint. Have you established a clear destination for yourself and all of your associates? Are you constantly tracking and monitoring the course your organization is taking? In addition to paying attention to your own controls, are you also seeking outside consultation from experts, as a pilot does with various controllers? Are you willing to reroute your organization during the mission if you discover you are off-course?

It would seem that many CEOs do not ask these questions regarding their business because they simply do not want to consider such issues. But as the pilot of your organization, you must be able to define the destination point of each mission you choose to fly. It is critical to determine whether your current course is leading you to the desired destination and whether or not the existing economic/market conditions justify taking off in a new direction. Again, you are the pilot. In aviation, it's clear that everyone who steps onboard with you will land in the destination that the pilot has charted and determined. That's also the case with your business.

Think about that. It's an awesome responsibility that scares some leaders and inspires others. Wherever you point that plane, all of your associates will generally follow. You can't simply show up to work each day and expect your company to reach your desired destination without real scrutiny and planning. Even simple operations—like short flights—require good planning and feedback. Having a clear vision is vitally important each day. In business, I have seen many people called to lead an organization walk into the office at 7:30; grab their cup of coffee and read emails for an hour or more; oversee several meetings that could be handled by others; check emails again or return phone calls; sit down for lengthy lunches; chit-chat with employees at the water cooler; and notice at the end of the day that they have not accomplished any real objectives. It's vital as a business leader (pilot) to avoid distractions and to keep the company on track to reach its destination. There must be a crystal clear vision of where the leader desires the organization to go. Otherwise, we are merely flying our business and our associates on a ride that will end at no particular destination and yield very little in the way of rewards. In addition, those called to follow a leader must both understand and personalize the vision. In other words, those following must own the vision in a way that their behaviors are tied directly to achieving the vision.

HOW TO MAKE VISION PERSONAL TO THOSE YOU ARE CALLED TO LEAD

First, make the vision about something much bigger than simply growth and profitability. Focus the vision on how your product and services will improve the life of others. Make your vision compelling and stirring to a man's soul. As noted architect Daniel Burnham said (drawing from the poet Goethe), "Dream no small dreams, for they have no power to stir men's blood. *Make big plans; aim high in hope and work...*" By aiming high and dreaming big, your team members can then feel that the work they are doing helps improve the life of others while stirring up the passion to be part of something great. Working to help others is a gift from God that is hard-wired in all of us. There are few greater joys than realizing we have made a difference in someone's life. We live in a consumer-oriented economy that sells the message that we can all find happiness if we only consume more. We fill our lives with things and busyness hoping to satisfy the eternal longings of our hearts, and in the end we find emptiness. Believe me, your people are looking for purpose in their lives. They have seen and felt the emptiness of consumerism and, like you, have found that more stuff has not necessarily led to happiness. Tailor your bold vision to be "other" focused—based on helping others—and I think you will find an almost immediate increase in energy (assuming the leader has provided great communication of the new/refined vision).

Our firm's vision statement, which our leadership team created years ago, is: "We honor God by stewarding resources, cultivating relationships and building extraordinary communities that enrich lives." The vision statement reminds us that our work is a way to honor God, and we do so in three primary ways—by being good managers of the assets we are given in business, being relationship-focused in all matters and building extraordinary places for people to live and work. The statement describes our passion as a faith-based company that sees work as a way to honor our Creator. We believe that we really can impact others both by how we treat them and by creating extraordinary places. The vision has caused our people to work with passion in the interest of others and in a way consistent with our business objectives. Develop a vision and purpose statement that calls to the heart of those you lead and you will find your team more inspired each day.

Second, tie compensation to the vision for every person in the organization. This one is challenging to implement but worth the effort. We all desire to be paid well for what we do. Compensation studies have shown that compensation is not the most important factor in retaining people, but I am convinced that paying people properly in terms of current and deferred compensation is a critical factor in upping the energy of a firm. Tying long-term compensation to achieving the vision of the organization helps align the team with overall goals. However, you must evaluate the value of each person's contribution as well as the person's need for current compensation. I have had senior executives who need higher current compensation than other similar level executives who are able to live on less in exchange for higher long-term rewards. It is important, I believe, to tailor compensation individually as much as possible so long as the system you have developed rewards each person in the organization for achieving the mission. A fairly applied compensation system will help increase the energy within the organization by tying each person's short- and long-term compensation to the company vision. The use of a firm that specializes in compensation studies is a valuable tool for all leaders, as it helped us adjust our leaders' pay to a system more aligned with our overall goals.

Chapter 14

The Equipment: Your Organization

In flying, the equipment you fly is critical to achieving the mission. Having the right plane for the objective is imperative. For example, if my desire is to fly to Dallas from Houston in a reasonable amount of time (under 2 hours) and carry one or two passengers, then a Cessna 182 single engine is a great fit. The 182 will carry up to four people and some bags and has a cruising speed of about 140 knots (161 miles per hour). However, if I needed to fly to Los Angeles with three people, the Cessna 182 would not be the ideal plane for the mission. We would not be able to carry much weight (baggage) beyond the passengers, the plane would be cramped for the occupants and the cruise speed would make for a very long flight (more than 7 hours with one or even two fuel stops depending on the weight of the passengers, weather and other factors). Conversely, a small jet like a Cessna Bravo would make the trip in a few hours and could easily carry the passenger load. While not rocket science, this has clear application to business—the business entity needs to fit the desired mission.

Having the right tools makes most jobs much easier. Having the right business structure makes accomplishing the business mission much more likely as well.

Planes come in a variety of sizes, shapes and ages. Sailplanes (also known as gliders) have long wings, which are designed to create a high level of lift to allow the plane to climb easily with rising air. The critical design feature of a sailplane is lift, which makes it less suitable for carrying large amounts of weight or for long cross-country trips. A two-person sailplane is designed to allow a pilot and one passenger to be towed into the air by a tow plane and then to climb via rising air without the aid of a motor. It is a very specific design created for a specific mission. Likewise, an aerobatic plane is designed for a mission far different than a commercial airliner. The aerobatic plane is designed for very short flights and maximizing control sensitivities so that the pilot is able to make the airplane fly in a variety of attitudes. Many high-performance planes, such as aerobatic and military planes, are deemed to be dynamically unstable, meaning that the airplane's design requires significant input from the pilot for the plane to remain in any particular attitude, such as simple, straight and level flight. In other words, the pilot must expend quite a bit of energy and attention simply to fly the plane straight and level, as the airplane is designed for maximizing the flight attitude envelope. Contrastingly, planes ranging from commercial airliners down to the Cessna 172 are generally very stable aircraft designed for straight and level flight and require minimal pilot input for the airplane to maintain a particular attitude. Such a plane is deemed to be dynamically stable. The airliner is clearly designed for long-distance flight and for carrying a considerable amount of weight, unlike the aerobatic plane that carries very little weight and can only fly relatively short distances.

How does this apply to business? Design of the airplane is strategic to the flight mission desired. Is your business designed for the mission you envision? Can you carry enough fuel for the mission at hand? Do

100

you have the right people for the desired mission? Can your current team handle the unusual attitudes involved in a high-growth business, or is your current team better suited for a more stable, slow-growth business plan? As the pilot in command of your business, one of the most important tasks at hand is for you to evaluate the organization and compare the assets of the organization to the desired mission. You are the corporate designer, no different than the aeronautical engineer who designs the high-performance aerobatic plane. You are responsible for designing the right organizational structure to achieve the desired objectives. Failure of the organization to achieve the mission falls to the designer—you as the CEO/leader.

One of the things Milton Schopper (my CEO coach) has told me repeatedly over the years is, "The company is perfectly structured to produce the results it achieves." I have this quotation on my desk and I read it each day. It reminds me that the results of our company ultimately fall to me as CEO. The lack of whatever resource we need ultimately falls to me. I am responsible for making sure we have the right design for the mission. I can cast all the vision I want, but if I fail to create the right platform to fly the desired mission then we will fail. Our people can do their very best, but if I fail to design the right organization then their work will never satisfy the goal. Thus, a critical role for every CEO/leader is to assess the strengths and weaknesses of their organization on a continual basis and compare the current organization to the desired mission objectives. Does the design match up to the mission that must be flown? Do I have a four-seat plane trying to carry the load of a commuter jet, or do I have a large tanker trying to do aerobatics? Match the design of your organization to the mission.

Within the overall design of a plane are critical components that can be applied to business principles.

AVIONICS

A key consideration of any airplane is the avionics or "panel" found within the airplane. Over the years, technology has rapidly changed the look and certainly the capability of most airplane panels. In particular has been the advent of so-called "glass cockpits" meaning the addition of computerized displays, which, at a minimum, consists of an MFD (multi-function display) and a PFD (primary fight display) and uses a "GPS" navigation system. The effects of having a glass cockpit over having six basic instruments by which to navigate and keep the airplane upright, as we had in the past, is an amazing improvement for the pilot.

The move to GPS navigation has been a landmark change in aviation. GPS navigational systems appeared in cockpits initially as hand-held devices but now have become a permanent part of airplane instrument systems. GPS systems are one of the most significant safety enhancements in flying over the past 50 years. GPS systems significantly (if not completely) eliminate the need for paper maps and the comparison of instrument readings to paper maps. The result is increased situational awareness and additional time in the cockpit for the pilot to perform other critical functions besides navigation. The GPS system virtually ensures that a competent pilot will not get lost or miss an airport. GPS navigation has in essence eliminated a pilot from being unaware of the plane's location relative to the ground. With GPS, the ability to determine course is a simple process and the ability for pilots to comply exactly with various controller-required procedures is a significant enhancement in safety.

The improvements in navigation equipment from one generation of technology to the next demonstrate the flying community's emphasis on finding better solutions. Each improvement in navigational technology has had a significant impact on flying safety and efficiency.

So how is your business/organization doing in situational awareness? What type of avionics is your firm using to know location relative to the desired goal? Do you and the leadership team have a clear picture of where your organization is relative to the goals you have established? Do you have a clear path (written strategy) and a clear destination in mind (written goals) that provides the basis for which to compare to your current position? How often do you receive situational updates? A pilot who is not really sure where the plane is flying relative to the desired course may blindly fly into a variety of harmful issues, such as rising terrain (mountains come to mind) or perhaps into the flight path of another plane.

Another by-product of not being sure of the plane's location is increased stress on the pilot as the pilot works to determine the plane's actual location. I can recall my early days of flying instruction that required I take a "long" solo cross-country before I could earn a private pilot's license. The time of my training was before GPS receivers, so I was flying by the paper charts and older navigational equipment. I chose to fly from Houston (KDWH—Hooks Airport) to Lufkin in east Texas, then to Huntsville and then back to Hooks. My flight path would take me near my parents' retirement home north of Tyler (the site of my fateful Thanksgiving flight many years later), so I planned to take a flight over their home on the second leg of my journey. After a successful flight to Lufkin, I departed Lufkin to the north with my paper maps in hand, intent on finding the small Holly Lakes community north of Tyler. As I flew north, I began to lose the visual references that I was hoping to see on the maps, and the problem was compounded by only being able to pick up one ground-based transmitter, which limited my ability to determine if I had ventured off course.

Today, the flight would be a simple navigational exercise with even the oldest of equipment, but when flying my first long, solo cross-country, the adrenaline was rising as I realized I was off-course but not sure of the course I should take to make it to Holly Lakes. I made the decision to turn around and head back to Lufkin. However, by now, I was sufficiently disoriented and unsure of the course to return to Lufkin. After flying aimlessly for a number of miles and sweat becoming more apparent as I contemplated the risk that I might be flying into one of the military operating areas depicted on my charts in nearby Shreveport, I was able to gain clarity on my location from the visual identification of landmarks on my paper maps. The mere understanding of where I was located relative to my desired destination brought my stress level down from the ozone and gave me renewed confidence in my ability to navigate my way back to my home base in Houston successfully.

Our business and organizational experiences are very similar. We often experience great stress simply because we are not sure of our firm's location relative to the desired course. Organizational stress can be greatly reduced simply by hitting the "pause" button and taking a current assessment of location. When the company appears to be off-course, and stress and fear are rising, leadership should call a meeting to discuss the firm's performance and direction. As I write this chapter, earlier today our leadership team completed a mid-year assessment of our company's performance as a whole and by business unit. My stress was greatly reduced by the end of the meeting as each leader discussed each unit's performance. In fact, as I write this particular section of the book, my attitude about our business is much more favorable than just a few hours ago, simply because I have better clarity on our company's position relative to the stated goals we have for the year.

Navigation in business and leadership starts with having clearly defined goals (destinations), and successful navigation (leadership) requires regular reviews of the firm's current position against the desired destination. The distance and location of the strategic destination compared to the current location gives the leader(s) the opportunity to change course headings as necessary (revise strategies) to get the organization pointed in the right direction. In our meeting today, as each business unit leader presented an update on current performance against stated annual goals, the balance of our leadership team was able to ask questions and suggest strategy for moving the business unit onto a course that would lead to obtaining the desired annual goals. Such "mid-course" correction is a great process to implement in any business or organization, and the discussion among your leaders is worth every second of time spent holding the meeting.

Like aviation, businesses and organizations need up-to-date navigational systems that provide critical information necessary for successful outcomes. To have a "glass cockpit" full of data, the modern leader needs to develop information systems that feed the critical data to all decision makers. Computerized accounting systems, order systems, HR systems, mobile applications and other software and hardware combinations have created the ideal environment for the effective leader to develop, design and utilize real-time data. If your organization's financial reports, customer information or other critical data is lagging behind what is necessary to make informed navigational decisions, make correcting those systems a priority.

A key tool for having current, up-to-date information is the use of "flash reports." I have found the development of "flash reporting" and other key dashboard indicators an extremely important part of piloting a successful organization. What do I mean by flash report or dashboard? I mean reporting systems that tell you and the leadership team on a regular, reoccurring basis how the organization is doing relative to agreed-upon key metrics and objectives. Is the organization in good shape in regards to working capital (fuel)? Does the company have adequate bank line reserves for a new project? On and on the list goes, but suffice it to say that your organization needs real-time information no different than a pilot needs real-time engine and navigational information in an airplane. The flash report should be provided weekly or biweekly to each leader and should have the information necessary for leaders to make decisions in the coming week that ensure their unit stays on the right course. Information can include a salesperson's production, accounts receivable, accounts payable, cash balances, deals closed, number of months' working capital, etc. The key is to develop a system that automatically populates a report with the information you need to evaluate your organization's health and progress toward its goals.

FUEL

In the glass cockpit environment, real-time data on the airplane's engines fills a number of screens with key figures on such items as fuel flow, gallons of fuel in the tanks, fuel required to the destination, fuel that will remain once the plan reaches the destination, cylinder head temperatures (piston engines), exhaust gas temperatures and voltage being generated to charge the batteries. Such data keeps the pilot well-informed on the health of the engine so he knows well in advance should there be anything catastrophic happening with the engine. Understanding fuel flow and gallons remaining upon landing is incredibly valuable for eliminating "fuel starvation"—one of the main causes of airplane crashes in the past. Today's information systems have made it far less likely for a pilot to not reach a desired destination due to simply running out of fuel. Inputting the gallons on board into the computer system after the plane is fueled or confirming gallons on board after engine startup allows the pilot to know with great certainty how much fuel will likely be on board at the destination based on the computer's calculation of fuel burn.

In business, fuel is often related to working capital and people. Having enough capital to reach our desired destinations is a critical factor. Too little capital and failure to manage that capital has killed many a company. It is the business leader's responsibility to ensure the right systems are in place to monitor cash flow on a real-time basis. The lower the organizational working capital (fuel), the more frequently the leader (pilot) must look at the fuel quantities and compare to the fuel required for the destination. If your organization is tight on working capital, it is even more critical that you (not someone else) ensure you have real-time data on working capital. I would go so far as to say that a business with very minimal working capital reserves should have cash flow information provided to the leader(s) at least weekly, or even daily if liquidity is extremely strained.

ENGINE TEMPERATURE

Another key information point for pilots relates to engine component temperatures. Depending on the engine type and the monitoring devices installed in the plane, key temperature readings in piston engine airplanes include cylinder head temperature (CHT) and exhaust gas temperature (EGT).

Engine temperatures relate best in business to the stress and anxiety of the people we lead. The higher the stress in an organization, the more likely the engine of the entity (the people collectively) will fail. In flying piston engine planes, the best ways to reduce high CHT and EGT readings are to add fuel, reduce power, slow the propeller and open the engine compartment air vent. In business, we can reduce stress in a number of ways, but the following are strategies I have found effective:

- Hold regular meetings with the company as a whole to state where the company is headed and how we are doing— whether good or bad. (Your folks know when the plane is in turbulence, so no need to deny the reality of rough weather.)

- Smile. Nothing makes people more nervous than to see the person in charge coming unwound. As a high-D personality, my natural tendency is to be intense under pressure. But I have learned over the years the importance of managing my emotions and expressions so as not to create undue alarm in those I am leading.

- Make time for fellowship. The simple act of breaking bread together as a team or company cannot be underestimated. Having a meal together is one of the most effective ways I know to get people to bond. From planning company-wide off-site retreats to casual lunches with coworkers, all are effective means of building trust and reducing uncertainty and stress.

- Have fun. Coach Slocum likes to say that the most important part of the word "fundamental" is the first three letters: "fun."

It is important for you and your team to have fun. Failure to have fun at work can lead to increased stress and lowers performance. If your organization is stuck in the mud and failing to meet objectives, you may want to hit the pause button and do something spontaneous. I remember a number of years ago taking our entire company to the movies on a Friday afternoon to see *Remember the Titans.* I had seen the movie earlier in the week and thought the story was a great illustration of teams working together to overcome challenges. At that time, we were struggling in several areas, but particularly in the area of team effectiveness. So without notice, I told all our associates (we do not use the term "employees" as it seems too legal to me) that we were going to the movies that afternoon and it was mandatory for each person to attend. Our people left the theater rejuvenated. I had our people discuss the movie afterwards, and the benefits of that spontaneous act of having fun as a team is still talked about today.

Good leaders understand the mood and stress level of the people they are called to lead. These leaders recognize when it is critical to lead aggressively and with great intensity and when it is better to lead the way through laughter, good memories and the fellowship quality of being together. Make sure you take time to stop and evaluate the mood of your team. If too intense and uptight, the company/ organization's results will suffer. Being too casual in the office can also lead to poor results. The effective leader has to discern what is going on with the people they shepherd and how to implement events that will help bond the team while reducing stress. It is critical that the engine temperature of your organization, the people, not heat up in a super-charged environment, as the long-term effect can be disastrous to your organization, just as a regularly overheating cylinder head in a plane can cause the engine to lose power and even cease operating—not a good thing if you happen to be flying at night over rough terrain in a single-engine airplane.

INSPECTIONS

The condition of an airplane can be very deceiving. From the outside and at distance, most planes appear to be in very good condition. In fact, most planes that are kept in service are in very good condition compared to their relative age. Unlike automobiles, which are kept outside much of the time, most airplanes are kept in hangars designed to minimize the impact of the elements on the plane's condition. The paint and other surface materials tend to last a very long time on well-maintained airplanes. The same is true of the interior conditions, as careful airplane owners make sure the interior is kept clean and well-maintained. As planes age, though, the exterior and interior, like most things, will begin to show wear. Careful inspection of the plane will reveal issues (often called squawks) with paint, tires, brakes and a host of other usually small items.

Unlike automobiles, piston airplanes are subject to annual inspections performed by licensed mechanics trained specifically for airplanes. Such mechanics have to pass both oral and written tests and have a minimum of 18 months' experience on engines or 30 months on both airframe and engines. The annual inspection of the airplane includes significant review of all major components and often requires the removal of the plane's interior to inspect all critical parts. To say the least, an annual inspection is a highly invasive procedure designed to ensure the airplane has no major issues that would render the plane unsafe. The mechanic also checks any airworthiness directives ("AD") that have been issued by the manufacturer of the plane and its components. An AD is simply a notice that a part on the plane has an issue that needs to be corrected. Some ADs are very easy and inexpensive to comply with and some are substantial and very expensive to implement. Again, governing agencies place safety at the top of the list. Put differently, they put achieving the plane's mission as the primary objective. Having a plane crash due to bad parts or a faulty issue that could have been repaired is not an acceptable outcome to those charged with airplane safety.

In our companies, how often do we have inspections performed to evaluate the condition of the firm? How about the health of the leadership team? Are annual physicals required for all who lead the teams in your company? Who is qualified to look at the business and assess the firm's condition? I have found that stopping to think about an organization's condition, particularly in light of the desired mission, is a challenging thing for most CEOs and other top leaders to accomplish. Why?

It seems that we get caught in the quadrant described by Stephen Covey long ago—urgent and important. As you may recall, Covey described four areas for how our time gets invested—urgent but not important, urgent and important, not urgent and not important and the fourth area—not urgent but important. Most top leaders have long ago learned how to stay out of the third box, but the first box is alluring. I say alluring because many of those same people are high-D leaders and love to live in the urgent. Living in the urgent gives high-D leaders a sense of purpose and a pace that fuels our adrenaline. We love the speed of a fast car or a roller coaster, and the same is true in how we like to lead. But, as I have already mentioned, with speed comes increased risk.

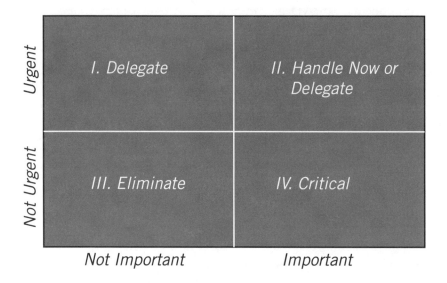

One risk that emanates from living in the urgent is the failure to ever spend time in the not urgent but important sphere. For example, the daily onslaught of email causes an undue amount of time to be focused upon requests for responses to a spectrum of issues, many such issues that do not rank as "important." Managing email effectively is one way to increase time available to focus upon more critical issues. Assessing the condition of the organization falls into the fourth box (not urgent but important) and requires the adrenaline-charged leader to stop and assess. It is brutally hard to do for many leaders, yet so vital. As we do with airplanes, I believe it is important for every organization to stop once a year and assess, among other things, the current condition of the organization. How are our people faring in the environment we have created (remember—the CEO is responsible for the culture)? Do we have the right people? Are our people worn out from long days and a heavy load? Do we need to add people to help lighten the load? Do we have too many people in a certain area? Do we have some people in the wrong seats needing to be reassigned to a new area? How is the engine running? Do we have good data, and have we taken time as a leadership team to stop and evaluate the data? Are we progressing in a positive direction? Is the organization running efficiently? What is our fuel burn (people turnover)?

Take time once a year to park the plane and evaluate its condition from one end to the other. Give your company an "annual inspection." You may even want to bring in an outside consultant to do staff interviews and give you a third-party status report. You may be surprised at what you find.

Chapter 15

The Weather

Behind pilot error, the number-two killer in aviation is weather. While some statistics argue that weather trumps pilot error as the number-one accident issue in aviation, it could be argued that a pilot does not have to take off and fly into bad weather, and most weather can be avoided once in flight. The reality is that most weather-related accidents are the result of pilot error, typically related to the pilot attempting to penetrate through weather that should have been avoided.

Weather involves all the external, environmental issues affecting an airplane and its mission. Weather can and does include things as simple as the sun and its impact on a pilot's visibility, to cumulus nimbus cloud formations that can tear an airplane to pieces if the pilot is not careful. The subject of weather is a primary area of study for all student pilots and should be a lifelong study for the serious pilot. Weather conditions can vary widely from one area to the next and, as such, it is critical to have a picture of what the weather will be at takeoff, enroute and upon landing. Failure to properly plan for each flight segment and the associated weather can lead to fatal results.

Weather information has never been more available to the pilot both prior to and during a flight. The same is also true for leaders assessing the environments in which their organizations must operate. The pilot today has satellite and other weather data available in the cockpit that provides current and forecast weather data both in narrative and visual form. Prior to a flight, a pilot using current technology can enter a desired flight plan on a personal computer, and the system will show the flight plan with current satellite weather depicted along the route. The pilot can do the same with forecast weather to get a very clear visual of the weather along a planned flight and can even obtain the same data in the cockpit while enroute to the destination. In planes equipped with modern glass cockpit screens, weather information is depicted on the displays, allowing the pilot to see the weather and its relationship to the planned flight route. In this day, there is absolutely no reason for a pilot to not have a clear understanding of the weather affecting the route.

Likewise, the business leader and most leaders today have access to an amazing amount of information typically only a few keystrokes away. General economic information to specific industry data can be obtained very quickly online. Our firm uses several research and data providers to give our decision-makers the most accurate data on the environment. We may not know exactly what interest rates will do in the next 12 months, but we can determine exact supply and occupancy information for a variety of real estate products in most every major U.S. market. We also can determine housing inventory in every major market along with the available vacant lots and other critical information. Such information was non-existent 20 years ago, but today the data fuels the mind of informed leaders in a variety of different business segments.

The key to obtaining useful data and getting a true picture of the "weather" surrounding your planned mission is having a process in place that regularly provides the key data you need to make decisions. If there is no repeatable system that generates the key data metrics then you will navigate only by happenstance. To set up this repeatable system, you likely will need to delegate the assignment to a detail-oriented, process-type person who has in their job description the requirement to provide the economic data for you and your leadership team. That data should include "weather"-related issues that need to remain in the forefront of the leader's mind as he works to steer the company. Such issues include:

AVOIDING TURBULENCE

Turbulence is a factor not generally associated with airplane accidents, but a weather condition that can definitely cause passenger and pilot discomfort. Most turbulence occurs near the Earth's surface as heat that has reflected off the surface rises upward. Unique turbulence can also occur around mountainous areas as the wind travels across the Earth's surface and is interrupted by the rising terrain of a mountainous area. This disruption of the airflow by the mountains can cause significant turbulence both in and around mountainous areas. Passengers in most commercial planes are well aware of mountain turbulence whenever landing in mountainous areas, particularly on hot days or days with strong winds. An interesting part of turbulence is that most of the bumps go away at a relatively low altitude (excluding turbulence found around very high mountains or associated with cumulous cloud formations). On any particular day, the bumps tend to end once the plane passes above the altitude of low clouds and/or the haze level. The turbulence generally tends to rise no higher than the lowest clouds. The pilot typically can eliminate the bumps by gaining altitude. Once above the altitude to which the disturbed air ends, there are typically few bumps found in the higher air.

The same is true for our businesses. As leaders, the lower we fly to the ground, the more bumps we will incur. By this I mean that the more we get involved in the daily grind, particularly personnel issues, the more we will find ourselves bumping around in turbulent air that is uncomfortable for everyone in the organization. The great leaders do not allow themselves to fly low for long periods of time but rather prefer to operate in the altitudes at which they are able to focus on strategy, setting vision and mission and making sure the organization has the resources necessary to achieve the mission. Leaders with less experience allow themselves to become involved in both non-leader personnel issues and tactical issues. Such focus can bring the leader down into turbulent air and carry the team along for the ride. For example, when an associate leaves the firm, perhaps damaging the company, does the lead person drop what he is doing to investigate all the issues surrounding the associate's reasons for leaving? If so, then everyone else on the leadership team will soon begin evaluating the reasons for the departure. The associate who left will become the center of attention for the organization, because the person with the vision pointer decided to descend and go after an issue that perhaps had personal impact or simply to right a perceived wrong.

I give this example because of my own recent experience with exactly this scenario. A young salesperson left our firm under some questionable circumstances. Because I had personally invested in the associate, I felt a bit betrayed by his actions. As CEO, I had plenty of advisers I could call for opinions and involvement, but instead decided to get involved personally. The net result was that I spoke some harsh words to the young man and I dropped our entire company into a personnel issue that consumed valuable time for several weeks. It was as if I put our firm into a nose dive down to 200 feet when the place was flying nicely at a 20,000 altitude. As our firm bounced along at a 200-foot altitude for all those weeks, our people were put through some very uncomfortable discussions about loyalty and commitment. In the end, I failed to stay out of the turbulence and instead brought the entire company into a turbulent period while I tried to right a wrong. The cost was ridiculous in terms of lost productivity and emotional investment, and the net gain was absolutely nothing. It would have been far better had I left the issue alone and let our unit leaders handle the matter.

As the leader or CEO, it is typically best to maintain altitude and stay out of the bumps other than for short durations. Let others handle non-leader personnel issues and other problematic items that you do not need to handle directly. Avoid the bumps by keeping altitude.

MANAGING IN TURBULENCE

In flying, sometimes due to fronts and other weather systems, it is not possible to climb high enough to clear the turbulence. In fact, some missions may have to be flown in turbulence. If the bumps are bad enough, the pilot is to reduce the speed of the airplane to a key speed called "maneuvering speed." Maneuvering Speed (Vm) is the speed designated by the aircraft manufacturer that will minimize the risk of structural damage to the airplane. Similar to boating when waves get large, it is best to slow down and ride up and down the waves of air instead of traveling at a high speed and bouncing off the waves.

The application of Vm to most organizations is a great strategy. When turbulence is encountered by your organization—*slow down!* In other words, when the company is having trouble of one kind or another—financial, personnel, strategy failures, etc.—take a step back and calm things down. How do you slow down? Put your capital in the bank and stop taking on new projects. Reevaluate your teams to ensure they are still working toward the strategic goals. If not, it may be the time to eliminate a business unit. Perhaps you have a few executives who are highly paid due to long tenures but their value-add has continued to decrease. In high-turbulence times, you may need to make tough decisions and lessen the weight in the organization. Sometimes for the good of the core team, you must let people go from a firm. The leader must keep in mind the strategic plan, which ultimately means keeping the airplane right side up and getting the passengers to a place where they can land safely—even if it is to a different destination. No one person's interest should be put ahead of the team. As an example, if necessary, the leader may need to remove a high-cost senior leader for the safety of the overall team.

Finally, during turbulence, the leader must ascertain the passengers' ability to stomach the bumps. In business, can your people handle a rough ride or do they need a break from a high-stress environment filled with uncertainty? As the leader, you must make the assessment about how long you can ask your people to hang on and when you must either climb out of the turbulence or land early to let your people regroup.

Chapter 16

Go/No-Go Decisions

Why do pilots continue into conditions that are not conducive to a high probability of success but instead take unnecessary risks, simply so they can land at a particular airport? The answer varies, but certainly one driving force is the need to be at a destination at a certain time. A private jet charter's crash while attempting to land at night in snow showers at the Aspen, Colorado, airport details one of the causes for pushing the risk envelope too far.

On March 29, 2001, a Gulfstream III business jet crashed into terrain while on instrument approach to Aspen-Pitkin County Airport in Aspen, Colorado, an accident killing the three crew members and fifteen passengers on board. Avjet Corporation, a private plane chartering company, operated the flight (and was held responsible for the accident).

After the captain and first officer had reported for duty and checked the aircraft and the weather, they left Avjet's facility in Burbank, California, and headed for Los Angeles International Airport (LAX) for passenger pick-up. While the plane was originally scheduled to depart at 16:30, late passengers delayed that departure for 40 minutes. And on the other end at the Aspen airport, a noise abatement curfew of 18:58 meant that the now-tardy flight would be cutting it close with an estimated arrival time just 12 minutes prior to the curfew's start. Not only that, but the FAA had given strict instructions that planes could not land at night at Aspen under instrument flight rules.

As the plane neared arrival and began the final approach with the appropriate step-down maneuvers requiring a fairly steep descent in the mountainous terrain, the pilots reached the missed approach point and continued their approach instead of diverting. It is important to note that several earlier flights had been forced to divert to other airports and were unable to see the runway environment at the missed approach point. At 19:01, the plane veered sharply left and crashed directly into the terrain, killing the 18 on board.

When the NTSB investigated the accident, it became clear that external factors had influenced the pilot's decision to land. The passengers who had chartered the flight insisted that the plane land at Aspen, going so far as to have Avjet called to actually *inform* the charter company that the plane would not be redirected. The reason? "The substantial amount of money that the [charter] customer spent for a dinner party." In addition, the cockpit voice recorder reveals the presence of a passenger in the cockpit, most likely giving strong pressure to the crew to land at Aspen.

In the case of the accident at Aspen Airport, the demands of a client caused the pilots to push too hard to make a landing in a very challenging environment, even to the point of violating FAA rules that the pilots knew were to provide an acceptable safety margin.

In our businesses and organizations, we are often pushed into conditions that are either beyond the organization's capabilities or beyond the leader's experience. I have led our firm into several new, seemingly opportunistic areas over the years. Once into the transaction or new venture, however, I discovered the conditions to be more challenging than expected. In such cases, we have generally aborted the mission and deviated to a new destination.

A few years ago, we were determined to get into the educational development area, building facilities for colleges and universities. We had landed a very nice piece of business with a local community college system and I felt we could duplicate the business in other areas of the state. I hired several senior people to lead and sell the business. But after two years of work, the guys leading the team hadn't been able to secure additional business, despite several different approaches. Like a pilot trying to land when the ceilings are just too low, we needed to abort and focus on areas where we could be successful landing new business, particularly our land development business, which had been expanding rapidly. As it turned out, the decision to focus on land development was very fortuitous, as the single-family home business began to improve rapidly in the Houston area.

The lesson is clear: when conditions are not as originally forecasted and after you have made several attempts to land, it is usually wise to abort the landing and go to another destination where the likelihood of success is much more probable. In my life I have learned that God opens doors and He closes doors, and that it is always best to pursue open doors of opportunity. Sometimes we have to be patient and wait for the right opportunities, always preparing and being ready for that particular open door that will lead to purpose and success. When I have attempted to force business to happen, like a pilot attempting to force a landing when ceilings are too low, I have only caused myself problems and disappointment. A quotation from long ago has resurfaced many times over the years, especially during a difficult business transaction: "You can work hard trying to make hard transactions/deals, or you can work hard finding transactions/deals that you can do." I believe it is best to pursue the second strategy of finding better conditions for a particular business segment.

Chapter 17

Instrument Conditions

One of the leading causes of general aviation fatalities is what is known as continued visual flight into instrument meteorological conditions.

The failure to control an airplane in instrument conditions generally can be linked to lack of pilot training in these kinds of conditions. The required training is mandated by the FAA and is called an "instrument rating." In essence, an instrument-rated pilot is qualified to fly in instrument conditions that require flight by instrument reference only, without visual reference outside the cockpit. What qualifies as instrument conditions? It is easiest to describe what instrument conditions are not. First, instrument conditions are not what are known as visual conditions. Visual conditions are those weather conditions for which all licensed pilots are qualified. Visual Meteorological Conditions (VMC) vary depending on the business of the airspace. In very busy flight areas (known as Class B airspace), visual flight rules require that a pilot can see three statute miles and remain clear of the clouds. In less busy airspace, the rule is generally three statute miles of visibility with a cloud distance of 500 feet below, 1,000 feet above, and 2,000 feet horizontally. Why is cloud clearance an issue? First, for avoidance of traffic that is flying in instrument conditions (clouds) and second because a pilot not trained to fly in these conditions can quickly become disoriented and lose control of the airplane, as noted in the previous accident. The reality is that marginal visual conditions can quickly turn into instrument conditions, and many a pilot has met their fate pushing the envelope in marginal visual conditions.

The Type-D pilot with a need to be somewhere, without instrument training or who has not flown regularly (and thus is not "current" as it relates to instrument flying), has and will make flying decisions that can end in fatality for himself and his passengers. The question is how to avoid ending up an accident statistic in flying or in business. The answer lies in two areas. First is to recognize that the pilot without an instrument rating and clearance, who still chooses to fly in marginal weather, had options other than to fly into conditions for which he was unqualified. The pilot could have aborted the flight and simply not flown the mission. The pilot also could have anticipated the possibility of conditions being worse than expected and then carefully planned ways out of the conditions, with survival being the number one goal versus simply completing the mission. And finally, the pilot could have committed the time (note the metrics—commitment and time) to obtain the training and experience necessary to safely operate an airplane in instrument conditions. The reality is that flying in instrument conditions can be as safe and likely safer than flying in visual conditions for a well-trained pilot who is operating per the regulations.

Similarly, flying a company into conditions for which the leader is not qualified and lacks a contingency plan can lead to disastrous consequences. The CEO or other leader who understands that the business climate is treacherous but continues to steam ahead, full of gusto and without a plan to abort should conditions decline, is no different than the pilot who continues visual flight into declining weather conditions. The business leader, like the pilot, must have a contingency plan in place for changing conditions. Likewise, the leader who chooses to lead the business or organization into bad conditions must have training and experience as to how best deal with a challenging environment. The instrument-rated pilot is well-trained to manage the flight into conditions where reliance on instruments alone is sufficient to complete a particular mission. Similarly, the business leader must be able to lead the company even when the "visibility" is low. In this sense, "visibility" refers to near-term, favorable economic conditions. Fortunes have been made and companies have moved to the "next level" in the midst of major economic storms because of bold, strategic leadership. In these cases, the leader must have the ability to access their organization's staying power, emotional strength and leadership ability to navigate through rapidly changing conditions.

STAYING POWER

The leader of an organization must understand and have access to the firm's financial ability to achieve the desired mission. No doubt, every leader and leadership team considers the financial stability within the firm. However, when the leadership is forced to fly the business in poor economic conditions, accurately accessing the firm's financial condition and staying power is essential. I mentioned flash reports earlier, and there is no time where flash reports are as critical as when the external conditions are shaky and the news negative. So many leaders blindly fly companies into bad conditions on the "hope" that things will simply return to normal in a short period of time. The quality pilot/CEO does not simply hope things will turn around.

Instead, the quality leader plans for and prepares the organization for possible issues should expected results not materialize in a reasonable time frame. The quality leader takes a long-term look at declining economic conditions and develops a mission plan that ensures the organization can weather even the longest economic downturn. The leader's attitude is focused on seizing the always-available opportunities in a downturn, instead of listening to the press and other "experts" who are shouting for everyone to take cover. It is one of the great thrills in business when as a leader, in the midst of a significant downturn, your firm has the economic staying power to create opportunities to grow your market share.

In 2008, the financial markets were in disarray and banks virtually stopped lending to real estate developers. The monetary crisis was significant and rapidly involved most of the world's economy. The U.S. banking system was teetering on the brink of a collapse not known since the Great Depression. To say there was fear in the marketplace would be a gross understatement. Every market was impacted by the withdrawal of credit from most every asset class. Real estate was particularly hard hit due to real estate's illiquidity and dependence on favorable economic conditions.

Within investment real estate categories, the two major types are income and non-income producing. Income-producing properties include office, retail, industrial, medical, hotel and a few others. The reason these types of properties are considered income properties is the users (for example, an office tenant) pay rent to the building owner. Thus the property produces cash flow from rental revenue and has the ability to service debt placed on the property. Conversely, non-income producing property, usually land, has no cash flow source. Land is the most illiquid of real estate assets and therefore the most challenging to finance for investment purposes. The financing of investment land requires the lender to look to the borrower for repayment should the land not sell or fail to be developed into an income-producing property. Banking regulators, therefore, consider land to be the most toxic of real estate assets. When the banking system was collapsing in 2008, land was the most impacted of all asset categories. But an interesting thing happened in the period from 2008 to 2011: income properties, for the most part, held their values due to the declining interest rate environment and the investor's desire for "safety" in hard assets. That is to say, in many cases, investors favored income property over stocks and other traditional assets; therefore, the income property market did not decline much. Land, on the other hand, represented a dark and foreboding environment in the 2008–2010 period, as banks in general would not finance the acquisition of land and investors were seeking yield from income properties.

As our team looked at the markets in 2008 and 2009, it became apparent that land represented the best investment opportunity many of us had seen in our careers. The question was how long would one have to hold the land and how would we capitalize the acquisition of significant land parcels at a time when both banks and investors were running from land. The solution rested in finding investors who appreciated value investing—that is, buying something that is likely worth a hypothetical dollar for a fraction of the value in a normal market. I have long been a value investor, and my goal in buying any asset is to ensure that we acquire the asset well below our determined market value. I do not care what others think about the asset's value, only what our team determines given our understanding of the market. In this case, we rule out outside opinions and instead rely on our own internal analysis so that we can make a decision based on analytics, not fear. To say the least, our shop runs numbers like crazy.

I am analytic at heart, and having numbers that show multiple possible outcomes helps evaluate downside risk and our ability to hold an asset through an extended downturn. In 2008, we began buying land and through 2011 increased our land holdings in the Houston close-in suburbs to over 4,000 acres. In only a few years' time, the result has been the creation of a significant asset base that has more than doubled in value as the markets have returned to more normal conditions. We were, however, prepared for the markets to take much longer to return to normal valuations—even up to ten years in some cases.

The point is, we made a decision to fly our company on a mission that to outsiders at the time looked very risky. However, because of our excellent team of analysts and brokers, we were able to identify quality assets that we felt would generate excellent returns once the markets returned to some form of normalcy. Fortunately, the markets returned to a condition that was as good as pre-2007, leading to a significant capital return for our company and investors.

EMOTIONAL STRENGTH

The emotional strength of the leader is paramount in all occasions, but none is more important than when the weather is rough. A favorite Biblical event of mine is when the disciples of Jesus are caught in a storm while in a small boat on the Sea of Galilee. The disciples had gotten into the boat to travel from one side to the other at the request of their leader, Jesus. However, as the boat made its way into deeper water, a storm suddenly came upon the group and the seas became threatening. The lives of the men were in danger, and in such a situation they turned to their leader. What was Jesus doing at the time of this significant storm? I will let Matthew, one of the men in the boat and a Gospel writer, tell you the story:

Then He got into the boat and His disciples followed Him. Suddenly a furious storm came up on the lake, so that the waves swept over the boat. But Jesus was sleeping. The disciples went and woke Him, saying, "Lord, save us! We're going to drown!" He replied, "You of little faith, why are you so afraid?" Then He got up and rebuked the winds and the waves, and it was completely calm. The men were amazed and asked, "What kind of man is this? Even the winds and the waves obey Him!" (Matthew 8:23-27, NIV)

Where was Jesus as the storm was taking over the boat? Was He jumping up and down like a madman, screaming for the men to row? Was He berating His men for getting Him into this mess? Coach Slocum has shared with me several times that a coach who is out of control on the sidelines will send a very clear message to his players that is not beneficial to them playing under control. It is hard to expect our players to remain calm, when we as leaders are acting out of control due to pressure. The strong leader keeps under control even when things are not going as planned, and even when the waves are rocking the boat severely. Jesus was so calm that He was able to sleep during a building storm. Why? Because He knew that ultimately the wind and the storm would subside at His command. Now, we certainly do not control the wind and waves like God, but we do have the power to trust in God's provision for our lives. One of the things I have found in strong leaders is a trust in God. I am not sure I have ever met a great leader that was not a faithful person. Oh, I have met strong leaders, men who will charge the mountain and certainly even take those mountains in some cases. But the men I know who are able to weather the storms of life and lead people on a path to greater purpose are all men of faith—period.

Emotional strength can be directly tied to faith. No self-help program or power of positive thinking will substitute for faith when the winds are howling and the plane is headed into unforeseen weather conditions. No, the faithful leader trusts not in his own ability for inner strength, but in God for His strength to be shown to all those being led. Like a mirror reflecting the noonday sun, so is a Godly leader who reflects the peace of God when the weather of life is rough.

NAVIGATING IN RAPID-CHANGE ENVIRONMENTS

One of the traits of long-term successful pilots and leaders is the ability to navigate quickly through rough weather—or as some like to say, "to think on their feet." The best-made plans may, at times, prove not to be the best strategy when external conditions change significantly from the forecast.

Successful pilots and CEOs share a common trait: the ability to navigate the unexpected. This trait doesn't appear out of nowhere and, in fact, comes from a combination of factors that I have found typically include the following: experience, training, emotional stability and faith.

No doubt experience plays a key role in a leader's ability to handle the pressures associated with guiding an organization through rough skies. There is no substitute for the accrued learning that comes from having been in similar past situations. Great athletes offer their best play and perform at very high levels when the game is on the line. Usually, though, this best effort comes simply because they have played in many other similar pressure-packed games and moments. The same is true for pilots dealing with rapidly-changing weather or an equipment malfunction. If the pilot has many times experienced the pressure of a rapid change in flying conditions and handled the issue well, there is a likelihood that the next time a significant unexpected change happens, the pilot will be able to react in a favorable manner.

One reason the commercial airlines safety records are so much better than general aviation (almost 4 to 1) is that a pilot must work his way up through the ranks, flying "right" seat as a co-pilot for an extended period of time and in each airplane type. Thus the pilot has learned by watching other more experienced pilots handle pressure-packed environments.

Like a mirror reflecting the noonday sun, so is a Godly leader who reflects the peace of God when the weather of life is rough.

The same would be true for business leaders. In the ideal world, the business leader would have been in an environment that allowed him to observe and assist other more experienced leaders make decisions in the heat of battle. I was fortunate to play football for three head football coaches during my five years at Texas A&M—Emory Bellard, Tom Wilson and Jackie Sherrill—and one future head coach. Our linebacker coach and defensive coordinator at the time was R.C. Slocum, who later would become head coach at Texas A&M and have one of the best all-time records in Division I football. I say that I was fortunate to have played for these four men in that I learned from each of them by observing their leadership styles. Each had his own style and his own way of dealing with pressure.

In business, we often face situations we never could have predicted. I can say that most times I have handled such situations well because of my faith that God is in control. There have been some times where

I have become angry and aggressive due to a bad situation, and in every case I so wish I could rewind the tape and get another shot for a better response. In the Bible (James 1:2-4), we are instructed to "consider it pure joy, my brothers and sisters, whenever you face trials of many kinds, because you know that the testing of your faith produces perseverance. Let perseverance finish its work so that you may be mature and complete, not lacking anything." I love this passage as it reminds me that with trouble, the faithful person develops perseverance, which leads to maturity. Through trials we learn to cope and mature as we work to find ways to operate in suboptimal (as we see it) conditions. The great benefit of these times is that we learn to trust someone outside ourselves. I believe with all my fiber that it is God's will through trials and suffering that we would learn to trust in Him.

The quality leader, I believe, trusts in God during times of great turmoil. Through perseverance and unwavering faith, I have seen great leaders lead others in a way that is unmatched by mere human effort.

So when the winds start blowing in your organization, I suggest you turn first to prayer and ask God to guide you in your decision making. Trust in Him and the quality of your decisions will improve markedly, as the uncontrollable circumstances that bring anxiety will be replaced by calm.

Chapter 18

Fly the Plane

WHO IS FLYING THE PLANE?

In what would become a landmark accident, on December 29, 1972 at 11:42 p.m., Eastern Airlines Flight 401 crashed into the Everglades just outside of Miami, Florida. All passengers and crewmembers on board the aircraft (a Lockheed L-1011 Tristar) were killed.

The aircraft had contacted Miami approach control about a half hour prior to the accident, after a two-hour flight from John F. Kennedy International Airport in New York. Captain Robert Loft, a 30,000-hour pilot who had flown the Tristar since its introduction, was joined by First Officer Albert Stockstill and Flight Engineer Don Repo.

As the crew reviewed the landing checklist, the captain noticed that only the two main gear lights had illuminated, so he asked Stockstill to check that the landing gear lever had been moved into the down position, which was confirmed. Stockstill then alerted the captain that there was no nose gear light, and Repo began to troubleshoot to see if a faulty bulb was to blame. After notifying the tower that they had an issue with the landing gear, Captain Loft flew the airplane away from the airport at 2,000 feet over the Florida Everglades. As they began to troubleshoot the problem, Captain Loft instructed Stockstill to engage autopilot and then Loft began checking the indicator lights himself. He also sent Repo to the avionics bay to evaluate the nose gear's position by sight. When the crew determined that the nose gear was, in fact, locked down, they again contacted the tower for a vector back to the airport. The cockpit conversation just prior to the crash went as follows:

> *23.42:05: We did something to the altitude.*

> *23.42:06: What?*

> *23.42:07: We're still at two thousand right?*

> *23.42:09: Hey, what's happening here?*

> *[Sound of click]*

> *23.42:10 [Sound of six beeps similar to radio altimeter increasing in rate]*

> *23.42:12 [Sound of impact]*

Voice recordings reveal no desperation by the crewmembers, or even any detection of something unusual until just before the accident. So what went wrong? The first officer's computer had been improperly programmed and the autopilot was indicating that the altitude hold was engaged when in fact the aircraft was in a gradual descent. As the crew tinkered with a malfunctioning light bulb, the plane was slowly descending at approximately 200 feet per minute, which the pilots never noticed until seconds before impact.

As you read the famed (in airline safety studies) Eastern Airlines Flight 401 story, did you find yourself wondering about the cause of the accident? From the findings, we know that the autopilot altitude hold was disengaged and that none of the crew realized that the plane was in a slight descent while at a very low altitude (2000 feet). There was the distraction of the light bulb failure, which caused the crew to become fixated on whether the bulb was bad or if, in fact, the nose gear was down and locked. Not having the nose gear down and locked is a very big deal on an airliner, so the captain did the right thing to communicate with the tower and then move to an area away from the airport to troubleshoot the problem. Captain Loft was a very experienced pilot with over 30,000 hours, so it is clear that his experience and training led him to the correct initial step of moving to an area to troubleshoot the problem. However, in this case, he failed in one primary area: leadership. The light bulb was not the cause of the crash but became a distraction to everyone in the cockpit, including the person responsible for flying the plane: the captain. In this case, Loft should have delegated either the flying or the troubleshooting to one of the other crew members but not allowed everyone (including himself) to neglect flying the airplane.

One of the cardinal rules I will always recall my instrument instructor hammering into my head was the call to "fly the airplane." No matter what the trouble, the primary concern as a pilot is to maintain control of the plane. The crew of Flight 401 neglected this obvious mandate. There are other factors that could have helped as well. The captain could have requested a higher altitude—say 4,000 feet—to give the plane more clearance should they need altitude for some reason. But the main thing the captain needed to do was manage his team with clear delegation of roles in an emergency situation.

As CEOs and business leaders, we should consider how well we delegate during trials. Do we have a delegation plan in mind and on paper for the roles to be played during turbulent times? The good leader will write out a list of the key roles that need to be played during a crisis. You may not know every need during the crisis, but many needed roles can be forecast, such as cash management, market reporting, customer service/contact and other critical assignments. And if you are the CEO or lead person for your company, do what you have been hired to do: fly the airplane and keep your organization out of the marsh during distractions in the company or economy.

Chapter 19

Weight and Balance

A WEIGHTY DECISION

Before taking off, a pilot must calculate the weight and balance of his aircraft to make sure the plane stays within the appropriate load limits. On August 4, 2000, a Piper Malibu Mirage crashed shortly after takeoff as a result of miscalculation and overloading. That morning, the aircraft departed with the pilot, two passengers, their luggage and large dog, and completely full fuel tanks. A witness observed the plane struggling to climb as it took off along the upward sloping, 3,900-foot runway, barely clearing a six-foot fence. Soon after, the aircraft collided with a utility pole, the roof of a bus stop, and a brick wall 150 yards past the pole. All aboard lost their lives.

The airplane's load included: cargo (268 pounds), the pilot and passengers (627 pounds), and fuel (120 gallons, or 720 pounds). The plane's empty weight was 3097 pounds and its maximum takeoff weight is 4318 pounds. At time of takeoff, it was 394 pounds overweight. The NTSB noted that the commercial pilot, who had over 6,000 hours and 80 hours specific to the Mirage, had not properly planned for the trip. Because of the excess weight and resulting imbalance, the plane could not climb adequately—especially on a short runway that sloped upward.

In our companies, we must evaluate how much weight we can carry and still get enough "lift" for accomplishing the mission. I have often thought of this analogy the first quarter of each year. As our business has grown over the years, our practice is to hire people through the year and then start the next year with revised business plans based on the additional personnel. The first quarter has always felt like the takeoff sequence in flying. We work hard during that first quarter to get momentum in the year and to gain much needed profitability during those initial months. The profitability is much like the altitude being gained as a plane climbs. The more altitude a pilot has after takeoff, the more options exist should a problem arise. The closer one is to the ground when flying, the fewer options that exist in the event of a problem. Gaining profitability early in the year gives the CEO and leadership team far more options than if the business is bouncing along with little profit and a slow start—similar to being close to the ground in an airplane and struggling to gain altitude. In some years, I have felt that our organization is heavy with personnel and struggling to get off the ground. Sometimes we will continue the course as we feel that the revenues will come and we have the right people in the right places. Other times, though, after a slow start, we will reexamine the businesses in our holding company and see if there is any way to move people to more effective positions before setting our focus on cost cutting (dropping weight from the plane).

The movement of people is analogous to the other weight issue in flying—balance. Every plane has a center of gravity, the point at which the plane will balance when empty. In other words, if you could lift an empty plane with one finger, there is a point along the bottom of the fuselage where you could place your finger and the plane would balance perfectly. That point is the center of gravity for that particular plane. Each plane is designed with a loading chart and information necessary for the pilot not only to determine how much weight can be carried for a particular flight (the weight issue is always a tradeoff of fuel versus payload—meaning the pilot must trade fuel to carry more weight. The less fuel the shorter distance that can be traveled), but the pilot also must place the weight so that the airplane's center of gravity stays within a certain range—called the center of gravity (CG) range. As long as the pilot keeps the weight within the CG range and the weight does not exceed the weight limits specified in the pilot operating handbook for the airplane, then the plane is configured correctly as it relates to weight and balance. On the other hand, if the pilot loads too much weight in the rear of the airplane so that the plane's weight is out of balance (too much weight aft) the plane will not fly as designed even if the total weight is within the prescribed limits. In the case of an airplane that is out of balance to the aft, the plane will want to fly nose high. In such case, the plane could become difficult for the pilot to control, particularly on takeoff where the plane's nose would want to climb too early and too steeply. Such improper loading could result in a stall of the plane at low altitude and likely result in a crash.

Likewise, in our companies, a key factor is where we have the weight—which is almost always people. It is people who make the plane fly in business and a company's ability to gain altitude is often dependent on having the right people in the right seats, as Jim Collins articulated in *Good to Great*. Having the right people in the right seats provides balance for the firm. When the people are sitting in the wrong seats, oftentimes their dissatisfaction with their roles can cause significant turbulence with the firm's ability to fly its mission. If a company has too many people improperly placed, the firm may be unable to attain near-term profitability as it struggles with internal discord and inefficiency. I believe every CEO and leader should have a sense about the organization they lead, whether the entity is "firing on all cylinders" or bumping along the ground trying to gain lift. When the leader has this sense, the leader (not a committee) must then start evaluating options for gaining speed (profitability). The fastest route is through expense reduction, but a better route may be repositioning the personnel within the firm to achieve better balance for the desired mission.

A final point on weight and balance: it is generally better to travel light. By this I mean it is exponentially more valuable to have an organization that can respond fast and seize opportunities than to have a larger organization with multiple levels on the organizational chart that moves at a slower pace. In the rapid pace of the technologically advanced society in which we live, I believe it is more and more important to travel light in business. Ideas for traveling light include outsourcing, office hoteling (same office shared by several associates), home offices, joint ventures, and partnerships, to name a few. Traveling light by its nature says that the best performance can come when overhead is at the lowest level necessary to achieve a given objective.

One metric we review every month in our firm is the overhead burden for our companies compared to our cash working capital. The result of dividing our cash balances by the monthly overhead ("burn rate") is to keep a constant eye on our overhead. To this end, our hiring policies are set based on this calculation:

Green (okay to hire): 5 months or more of working capital
Yellow (hire only if critical): 3 to 4 months of working capital
Red (must reduce head count): less than 3 months working capital

Since we implemented the above system ten years ago, our leadership team has had a much clearer understanding of how heavily loaded our firm is for the missions currently being flown. With the month's working capital metric coupled with long-term graphical depiction of our overhead burn rate, every month we have an excellent mechanism to evaluate our firm's loading. Every firm should develop an appropriate measure of loading if it currently does not have such critical information available. Likewise, if you are at a light weight and still struggling, then take a hard look at moving people around to more effective roles.

Chapter 20

Dealing with the Unexpected

In preparing for departure, the seasoned pilot considers contingency plans should a problem arise during takeoff. Statistics prove unequivocally that the most dangerous flight segments are takeoff and landing. Both occur close to the ground, and both occur at lower speeds where the ability to climb is impeded or limited by the lack of significant speed. Statistically, takeoff is less dangerous than landing, but still a major area of concern should a significant problem occur during the takeoff portion of a flight. During takeoff, the airplane is close to the ground, requiring the maximum thrust to gain altitude, and resolution of problems is limited should the airplane be headed downward. Accidents during takeoff have been caused by everything from mechanical failure to doors opening to dogs jumping into the controls. Perhaps the most harrowing takeoff issue, however, is loss of power after the "point of no return."

What I mean by the "point of no return" is that moment during the takeoff run when the plane reaches a speed at which the remaining runway does not allow enough room for the pilot to shut the engine down and land or stop on the remaining runway. At some airports, running off the runway would not necessarily be a huge factor, provided the ground is relatively level and there are no obstructions at the end of the runway (such as a fence or trees). However, an airstrip like the one I described in my Thanksgiving flight out of east Texas is a different matter, with heavy trees and a fence lining the end of the runway. Commercial airline pilots actually call out speeds as they are making the takeoff run, and there is a speed of no return (after which the takeoff is not to be aborted) known as V1. After V1, the flight is to continue to takeoff regardless of conditions or other issues. Once the plane reaches the speed necessary for flight, known as Vr, the pilot will pull back on the stick and establish a climb attitude. The plane will then rotate (the "r" in Vr) and begin its climb.

The reality is that almost all takeoffs in a pilot's career go as planned. I suspect there are many pilots who have never experienced a takeoff issue during their entire career, other than in a simulator. The now infamous U.S. Airways Flight 1549 on January 15, 2009, well illustrates the point of expecting the unexpected. The pilot in command was 57-year-old Captain Chesley B. "Sully" Sullenberger. The flight was aboard a 1999 Airbus A320-214 powered by two GE Aviation turbo fan jet engines and was a routine flight from New York City's LaGuardia Airport (LGA) to Charlotte/Douglas airport in North Carolina. The events of the day were as follows:

> Shortly after taking off and passing through an altitude of about 2,700 feet on the initial climb, First Officer Skiles (who was at the controls of the flight when it took off) was the first to notice a formation of birds approaching the aircraft about two minutes into the flight. According to the flight data recorder, the airplane encountered the group of birds at an altitude of 2,818 feet above ground level and about 4.5 miles north-northwest of the approach end of Runway 22 at

LaGuardia. The windscreen quickly turned dark brown as the team heard several loud thuds as birds hit the airplane. Both engines immediately lost thrust. Captain Sullenberger took the controls while Skiles began going through the three-page emergency procedures checklist in an attempt to restart the engines.

At 3:27:36, using the call sign "Cactus 1539," the flight radioed air traffic controllers at New York Terminal Radar Approach Control (TRACON). "Hit birds. We've lost thrust on both engines. We're turning back toward LaGuardia." Passengers and cabin crew later reported hearing "very loud bangs" in both engines and seeing flaming exhaust. At this, the engines went silent and the passengers could smell the odor of unburned fuel in the cabin. Responding to the captain's report of a bird strike, controller Patrick Harten, who was working the departure position, told LaGuardia tower to hold all waiting departures on the ground. He then gave Flight 1549 a heading to return to LaGuardia and told Sullenberger that he could land to the southeast on Runway 13. Sullenberger responded that he was unable.

When Sullenberger first asked if they could attempt an emergency landing in New Jersey, mentioning Teterboro Airport (TEB) in Bergen County as a possibility, air traffic controllers quickly contacted Teterboro and gained permission. However, Sullenberger then told controllers that he couldn't do it, making clear his intention to bring the plane down on the Hudson River due to a lack of altitude. Air traffic controllers at LaGuardia reported seeing the aircraft pass less than 900 feet above the George Washington Bridge. About 90 seconds before touchdown, the captain announced, "Brace for impact," and the flight attendants instructed the passengers how to do so.

DITCHING

The plane ended its six-minute flight at 3:31 p.m. with an unpowered ditching while heading south at about 130 knots (150 mph) in the middle of the North River section of the Hudson River. Sullenberger said in an interview that his training prompted him to choose a ditching location near operating boats so as to maximize the chance of rescue. The location was near three boat terminals, and after coming to a stop in the river, the plane began drifting southward with the current.

NTSB Board Member Kitty Higgins, the principal spokesperson for the on-scene investigation, said at a press conference the day after the accident that it "has to go down [as] the most successful ditching in aviation history...These people knew what they were supposed to do and they did it and as a result, no lives were lost."

EVACUATION

Immediately after the A320 had been ditched in mid-river, Sullenberger gave the evacuate order over the public address system, and the aircrew began evacuating the 150 passengers. Two flight attendants were in the front, one in the rear. Each flight attendant in the front opened a door, which was also armed to activate a slide/raft. One rear door was opened by a panicking passenger, causing the A320 to fill more quickly with water. The flight attendant in the rear who attempted to reseal the door was unable to do so. It was later revealed that the impact with the water had ripped open a hole in the underside of the airplane and twisted the fuselage, causing cargo doors to pop open and filling the plane with water from the rear. The flight attendant urged passengers to move forward by climbing over seats to escape the rising water within the cabin. Having twice walked the length of the cabin to confirm that no one remained inside after the plane had been evacuated, Sullenberger was the last person to leave the aircraft.

Evacuees, some wearing life-vests, waited for rescue on the partly-submerged slides knee-deep in frigid river water. Others stood on the wings or, fearing an explosion, swam away from the plane. Air temperature at the time was about 20°F and the water was 36°F.

Notice the many steps that led to a very positive outcome. First was the flight crew's focus during takeoff on a day when few hazards were evident. In other words, the flight took place on a clear day with no apparent outside weather issues or conditions that might cause concern for the flight safety. The airplane's systems were all functioning normally upon takeoff and the plane was climbing as designed. However, as often happens in life, there was an event that simply could not have been anticipated. The flight of birds directly in the flight path could not have been expected or planned for as the pilots did their pre-flight checks. The crew responded to the loss of engine power in a decisive manner, indicating focus and attention at a time when others might have not been as attentive. Recordings of the pilots' voices reveal the steely focus of two veteran pilots who knew they had a very serious issue to address. The ability to stay focused and not panic was clearly the result of training and confidence in knowing the procedures.

Although no one could have predicted the miraculous, positive outcome, the pilots trusted in their training and procedures. When times get rocky in your company, do the people leading the business or a business unit have the training necessary to default to a proven set of procedures? Do we as leaders have a series of set tasks to perform if the business or business unit starts to experience severe challenges? For example, if we lose a major account that is responsible for perhaps the majority of the bottom line, how should leadership respond? What is the first, second, third and fourth step you or your leadership will take should you encounter the unthinkable? The answer lies in having thought through the unthinkable. Failure to plan for and develop contingency procedures around negative outcomes is negligence on behalf of the leader and the leadership team.

A good exercise for any CEO or leader is to run through a worst-case scenario with the leadership team on a somewhat regular basis (at least twice a year) and discuss what steps should be taken. What would you do first and why? The key is not that you will have exactly the right answer, but that when the unthinkable happens, you have a go-to set of decisions. A great leader can find peace in a storm if one knows ahead of time what the first couple steps should be. Plan a time with your leadership team to discuss the unthinkable and how you plan to move forward.

Second, the chief executive officer took control of the plane upon encountering a major difficulty. I cannot stress enough the handoff that occurred in the cockpit. First Officer Skiles immediately yielded control of the plane to Captain Sullenberger upon hitting the birds and losing the engines. Skiles knew he had a role to play and that was to work through the emergency checklist. I would point out to you that the most gifted and experienced pilot (the CEO) took control of the plane, while the understudy went through the processes necessary to deal with the emergency. When the company hits a major problem, the CEO should be leading decisively. Far too many times, I have observed CEOs who try to take a consensus leadership style into crisis and simply react too slowly to the rapidly changing external conditions. The academic world loves to stress the benefits of collegial decision making by soliciting the input of others and working through an inclusive process to yield a strong, team-supported decision. However, when response time is short and risk is high, team decision making needs to be terminated. The leader/CEO should turn to a limited few for counsel.

For me, in times of difficulty (and in times or prosperity), I turn to the Lord each day and seek His counsel, both in prayer and in studying His Word. Many times throughout my business career, I have read the Bible and prayed through the night about particularly challenging situations. In every case, God has provided the means and wisdom to navigate some very treacherous issues. For me, God is the first counselor, followed by my spouse, Susan, who has great discernment and is a great encourager. I think one of God's many blessings is to have a supportive spouse that can encourage us in times of challenge. Thirdly, I seek out trusted advisors that have specific experience relevant to the issue at hand—a quality advisory board should be a good way to fill this need. During the rockiest times of my business career, I have found it beneficial to limit the number of people that are speaking into my mind to ensure I hear only those that have relevant experience and wisdom.

Chapter 21

The Pilot's Logbook

One of the important requirements for all pilots is to record in writing (now automated via computerized logbooks) certain data on each mission, including the number of takeoffs, landings, how much of the mission was conducted in IFR weather, if the flight was conducted at night, how much time the pilot acted as pilot in command, and other information including a narrative summary of the flight. Such data is not only required to comply with the various FAA regulations but also are a great way for each pilot to review and remember flights and the lessons learned along the way. I can look back over my logbooks and see my flying history unfold page by page, including errors I have made in flying (the Thanksgiving flight is well-documented) and some of the amazing sights I have seen while traveling from place to place from the vantage of the cockpit. From incredible sunsets to towering cumulus clouds, reading through my logbooks reminds me of the amazing gift we have in flying.

Similarly, I also keep a personal and business log. My personal logbook sits by a large easy chair in my study at home. Each morning, I take time to write out what happened in the previous day and to consider the current day prayerfully. I make notes about what I am learning along the way and what God is saying as I study the Bible. I

153

note answers to prayers and circle items that are clearly signs that God is present and real in my life. Such "waypoints" are critical to me in remembering that God has His best intentions for my life regardless of circumstances and issues. As mentioned earlier in the book, I also keep a company logbook that I have used now for over 20 years to record my thoughts on each year's performance. I cannot emphasize enough the importance of that red spiral notebook in my leadership. Each year, I take time to review pages filled with notes about issues that arose in those previous years. I see my mistakes recorded so that I do not forget and I see good decisions made by our team that led to business and market success. I would encourage every leader to have a daily journal and a company/organizational logbook. In the end, life is very short, so being able to record the journey and remember both the highs and lows is a valuable part of being an effective leader. Lest I forget the many errors I have made along the way and think myself a better man than I am, the journal and corporate red book remind me to be very humble and thankful to God for His grace.

Before We Land

As I close this book, I want to thank you for taking time to read through my thoughts and ideas on leadership. I hope you will gain some ideas that you can implement in your business or organization. The leadership lessons learned in aviation have a direct application to leading organizations, and clearly the role of pilot can tie well to the role of CEO or business unit leader. The accidents I cited throughout the book are tragic in nature, yet they serve also to inform us as to how to make better decisions, whether in aviation or in leading an organization. From handling turbulence to ensuring that leaders have proper training, the aviation industry has created a model for completing successful missions, whether you are flying/leading the equivalent of a Cessna 172 or a Boeing 777.

I hope you have enjoyed the leadership lessons shared in the book. I pray you have many days of clear-weather flying and that when the storms arise, you are better equipped to handle the weather of the marketplace.

ACKNOWLEDGMENTS

I am blessed to have been surrounded by many great and faithful people my entire life. This book would not be possible were it not for the love and support of the people that have poured into my life.

I want to express my thanks to the following people:

Susan, my wife now for 32 years, has been a great catalyst in my life supporting me when few others would. Susan is an amazing woman that loves the Lord and has a heart for serving others.

My parents, Bill and Nancy Caldwell, created a family environment that caused each of my three siblings to focus on God and being the best we could be at whatever we chose to do. My parents were supportive of each of our varied paths and never tried to control our lives. They simply loved us well and let us develop as God intended. Susan's mother and step-father, Doris and Don Stallings, were a significant influence in my life. Don was a homebuilder in Houston and taught me much about business, the building business, the outdoors and life. Doris, is a wonderful lady who loves people, adventure and cooking a great meal. My life has been blessed by having two amazing sets of parents.

I am so proud of Amanda Grace and Lindsey Joy for who they are and their willingness to follow unique calls. Each has a strong faith and are Godly women. Amanda Grace will soon publish her first book, titled "Meanwhile" which focuses on her passion for counseling young women. Lindsey lives in LA and continues to pursue her dream of being on camera and using the stage as a platform for God's purpose.

In addition, I am very thankful for the many mentors that have graciously given of their time and lives to help me along the way. The list of people includes my good friend Ron Pugh, a very successful entrepreneur who sold his business a few years ago and became an even more important mentor. Ron's business acumen and read on situations is unparalleled among people I have known. Ben Reynolds was kind enough to hire me in the commercial development and investment business and taught me much about wise investing. I will mention him further in the book, but Coach R.C. Slocum has been a significant influence in my life since I was 18 years old. Chuck Watson, who invested in our company at a critical juncture, gave me a very good picture of the CEO role at a much higher level. Chuck has had an amazing ability to manage multiple executive roles while still ensuring the ventures he leads are very successful. Spiritually, I cannot thank Clois Smith, Bruce Johnston, Mac Ogren, Scott Thayer and Kevin Rudolph enough for their willingness to walk alongside me and disciple me in the ways of God. I also am indebted to David Sumlin who invited me to participate in the planting of a church and to assist in preaching for many years—a great blessing.

All these men are dear friends who have always been willing to provide me with invaluable counsel on a variety of issues. I cannot thank these men enough for their help and friendship.

Finally, I want to thank Mark Russell with Elevate Publishing for helping make this book a reality.

ABOUT THE AUTHOR

Fred Caldwell began his career with The Originals Group in 1983 and joined Southern Realty Corporation in 1985, becoming President in 1988. Fred was the founding partner of Caldwell Nyberg Interests in 1990, which was later renamed as Caldwell Companies. Today, the firm serves as a holding company for a family of related companies that invest in, develop, broker and manage residential and commercial real estate interests and participates in private equity investments.

Fred serves on the Board of Directors and was past Chairman of the Cy-Fair Educational Foundation, is a former member of the 12th Man Foundation Executive Board, is a Lowry Mays College & Graduate School of Business Development Board Member, is on the Board of Directors and was past Chairman for the Lonestar College System District Foundation, JH Ranch and Outback Ministries Board and is an Elder with Terra Verde Community Church. Fred is a graduate of Texas A&M University and holds both a Master of Science in Finance and a Bachelor of Science in Accounting. Fred was a three year letterman on the Texas A&M football team. Fred and his wife, Susan, have been married for 30 years and have two children, Amanda and Lindsey. The Caldwells reside in Northwest Houston.

elevate
publishing

A strategic publishing company empowering authors to strengthen their brand.

Visit Elevate for our latest offerings:
www.elevatepub.com